MW01451892

HIDDEN
Agendas
A T W O R K

'The GiCo Story'
From the Book
"Spiritual Intelligence at Work"

COLIN C. TIPPING

Copyright © 2007, Colin C. Tipping.

All rights reserved. No part of this publication may be reproduced, stored in a retrieval system or transmitted in any form or by any means, electronic, mechanical, photocopying, recording or otherwise, without prior written permission from the publisher and author, with the exception of short excerpts used with acknowledgement of publisher and author.

"Hidden Agendas at Work"

ISBN 978-0-978699-35-2

Originally featured in the book, "Spiritual Intelligence at Work, A Radical Approach to Increasing Productivity, Raising Morale, and Preventing Conflict." Published in July, 2004

Printed in the United States of America

The Quantum Energy Management System and **QEMS** are trademarks owned by Colin Tipping.

Published by Global 13 Publications, Inc.
26 Briar Gate Lane,
Marietta GA 30066

Websites:
www.radicalforgiveness.com
www.qemsystem.com
www.spiritualintelligenceatwork.com

Contents

Introduction	1
The GiCo Story	5
Humenergy Dynamics at GiCo — An Analysis	103
Using QEMS Technology For Our Own Soul Survival at Work	113
Contact Us	128

Author's Preface

The GiCo Story was initially featured in my book, *"Spiritual Intelligence at Work."* It was printed on the left-facing pages while the didactic material that outlined the rationale for the Quantum Energy Management System was printed on the right-facing pages.

While this was a successful strategy in that it made no judgment about which should run first and ensured that the story had as much chance of being read as the other material, I am excited to now be offering the GiCo Story as a standalone book.

I present it to the reader now not so much to make a particular point about spirituality in the workplace, which was its purpose in *Spiritual Intelligence at Work,* but simply to be enjoyed as a poignant human story. I think you will agree it is that.

It is simply about how we as human beings on the spiritual journey we call "life" create all the circumstances of our lives and enroll others into the game as healing partners. The workplace, it seems, is the perfect place to do it.

That said, however, this wonderful healing process should not occur to the detriment of the organization. In fact, what this story shows is that it can be to the great advantage of both the individuals and the organization if this dynamic is properly understood and managed. This is what the Quantum Energy Management System offers.

Enjoy the book!

Colin

Introduction

This is a story about a small company going through a major crisis. The company is basically sound but is seriously threatened by some latent, unconscious material of certain key personnel rising to the surface to be acted out as a way to heal it. I have coined the word ***humenergy*** to describe this unconscious, negatively-charged material.

Four forms of energy flow through any organization — **money, data, materials, and human energy.** Organizations have learned how to manage the first three, but have failed miserably on the fourth.

Accounting for up to 85% of an organization's overhead, human energy can be extremely volatile and unpredictable. *Humenergy,* with its origins in our childhood wounds and early learning, is especially dangerous, as you will see in this story.

Humenergy is dangerous, not only because it exists below the level of awareness, but because it will find a way, as part of the natural healing process, to come to the surface for release. This is healthy for the person, but it can be disastrous for the organization when that happens.

HIDDEN AGENDAS **At Work**

That people bring their *'humenergy'* to work with them and at crucial moments tend to act it out, is a fact of life. It is what human beings do. From the CEO to the lowest paid worker, everyone is prone to this process.

However, when *humenergy* does come up for healing it is cleverly disguised, even from the people themselves, as conflict, dissent, absenteeism, passive-aggressive behavior, self-sabotage, driven behavior, disloyalty and other dysfunctional behavior. That these can be seriously damaging to the organization as well as to the individual is well illustrated in the GiCo story.

Up to now this mechanism has not been recognized or acknowledged as a primary cause of conflict, low productivity, high attrition and low morale in just about every kind of organization. But in fact, the GiCo story is virtually every organization's story. It makes no difference what size it is, what kind of organization it is, what it manufactures or what service it offers; if there is more than one person involved, you will have *humenergy.* At some point it will come to the surface.

The purpose of this book is to explain the dynamics of *humenergy* and to show how it might easily be managed by enlightened and sensitive personnel within any organization. This can be done using simple tools that have already been shown to work well in situations where there is conflict and similar problems.

Once business owners and managers see how the use of these tools affects productivity and profits, they will quickly begin to install the systems like the one suggested in the story.

That's about as much as I intend to say prior to you reading the story. I want the story to say it all. However, there is some further analysis of *humenergy* in the Epilogue which shows how it worked with each of the characters in the story, one of whom is the CEO himself, and how it came close to ruining the company, not to mention a few careers.

Enjoy.

Colin Tipping

HIDDEN AGENDAS **At Work**

The GiCo Story

It was Bob's fiftieth birthday. Nevertheless, he was making his way to the office at his normal hour. He liked to be at his desk by 6:45 a.m. every day, which meant departing from home at around 6:15, leaving Jean and the two kids still fast asleep.

That way he could avoid the morning traffic and get a decent amount of work done before the general hubbub of the working day began with all its demands, pressures and distractions. Also, being something of a loner, he liked to have at least some part of the day to himself.

As usual Mrs. Harper, his secretary, arrived on time at 8:30 a.m. She was the only one who knew that it was his birthday. Bob had told her explicitly that he did not want a party or anything like that. Neither did he want anyone else to know that it was his birthday — especially his fiftieth. He didn't feel like celebrating anything, so he'd much rather it went unnoticed.

Bob was a little below average height with a slim athletic build. His hair was mostly thick and dark except for graying temples. You might not, at first glance, take him for fifty. Where he really did show his age, though, was around the eyes. Deeply set and ice blue, they were not at all easy to see beneath his bushy eyebrows, which were knitted into a perpetual frown — obviously the result of many years of stress and worry. His finely chiseled face and open smile made up for it though. He was really quite handsome.

Still, he was not feeling good about reaching fifty and didn't want attention brought to the fact. He just wanted the day to pass unnoticed, and to be like any other ordinary day. In fact, Bob was feeling more depressed than normal and didn't really know why. For the last six months he had been feeling very disturbed; as if something were gnawing at him from the inside.

He'd had similar experiences in the past but had always managed to push the feelings away by immersing himself in his work. As president of the company he always had a mountain of work that he never could get the better of, so it had always been easy for him to bury those feelings by working long hours.

This time it didn't seem to be working. Lately he was finding himself unable to really focus on his work, becoming indecisive and reclusive. He was biting people's heads off and being demanding, critical and really hard on the very people on whom he depended.

The **GiCo** Story

Throughout the company people were talking about the situation, and many of them were beginning to wonder whether their boss was really up to the job. It wasn't just affecting the senior management team who had to deal with him every day, but was trickling down the ranks and affecting morale throughout the firm.

In a company employing around fifty people there is still a possibility of there being something akin to a family atmosphere, especially when, as was the case with GiCo Inc., many of the employees had been there for several years, having been promoted up through the ranks. In GiCo's case, this had produced a loyalty and a synergy that had worked really well over the years. But, as with any extended family, if one part becomes dysfunctional, everyone senses it and a major disturbance results.

One such disturbance had occurred five years earlier when the man who had been president of the company for the last thirty-five years retired. Contrary to expectations, the board appointed someone from outside the company. That person was, of course, Bob Pearson.

There were at least two people at GiCo who had coveted that job for many years, both of whom probably would have accepted the appointment of the other with equanimity. So when an outsider was appointed, the two contenders were both flabbergasted and enraged.

HIDDEN AGENDAS **At Work**

They felt totally betrayed. One of them took early retirement and left. He died within the year.

Bob's appointment also split the company, since those loyal to the contenders were openly hostile to Bob and were uncooperative for at least the first two years. In many parts of the company the wound still festered, even after five years.

Dennis Barker, the other contender for the job that Bob landed, did not leave the company. As vice president of sales and marketing he was, in effect, Bob's number two; but it was clear that he considered himself superior to Bob, both in intellect and experience.

Dennis made an effort to be a good number two, but it actually wasn't in him to be satisfied with that position. He always wanted to be number one. Bob could sense the resentment that was just beneath the surface, and Dennis would covertly act it out. He would find ways to withhold important information from Bob or to subtly undermine him in the minds of the management team.

The sabotage was never overt enough for Bob to challenge him on it, for Dennis was too clever to leave himself open to that. But the passive-aggressive behavior was always there. He also never lost an opportunity to finesse Bob in a way that confirmed for himself — and for Bob too, probably — his superiority.

Dennis was physically overpowering as well. He weighed at least a hundred pounds more than Bob, and at six feet three inches, he towered over Bob, who was only five feet eight inches tall. Whereas Bob moved quickly and easily, Dennis was lumbering and slow by comparison; he also had a slight stoop.

Even though Bob never let it show, he despised Dennis. He couldn't stand Dennis' false servility and insatiable need for approval. He felt Dennis was inauthentic and untrustworthy and saw him as the stereotypical sales type — great on the surface but with little substance beneath. He saw Dennis as manipulative, self-centered and needy.

Bob did pretty well in disguising these feelings, and to an outside eye, their relationship might seem cordial and even mutually respectful. But those who worked closely with the two of them knew better. They could feel the energy between them, and it was not good. Though the situation drained energy from the team, no one mentioned it — at least not openly and certainly not to Bob or Dennis.

Meg

Meg saw her nine year-old daughter Caroline onto the school bus at 7:15 a.m. as she normally did, and then got back into the old Honda Civic she had managed

HIDDEN AGENDAS **At Work**

to buy from her brother a couple of months before at a really good price. He had upgraded to a new SUV upon getting promoted at work. Knowing that Meg was struggling to make it as a single parent with no child support coming from her ex-husband, he let her have the car on a monthly payment basis. She made the drive to work in about 40 minutes and arrived ready to start work at 8:00 a.m.

Meg, having started in the shipping department, had been with GiCo for almost 8 years and in that time had progressed up the ladder to become a production supervisor. She was well thought of by those she supervised and, with the exception of one person, by everyone else in the company.

The exception was Monty Fisk, the production manager. For some reason he had it in for Meg and, as her boss, was making her life miserable. Everything had been fine for the first three years. He would sing her praises and give her all the resources she needed.

Then suddenly, after she had been there three years, everything switched. From that point on nothing was ever right, not only with her but with all those she supervised. He found fault with them all at every opportunity. Meg frequently ended up having to defend her staff members against him. They loved her for it, but it put a lot of stress on her and only made her relationship with Monty worse.

The **GiCo** Story

He took every opportunity to load her up with additional responsibilities and then set her up to make mistakes so he could find fault with her. Every time an opportunity came up for a possible promotion for Meg, he blocked it. And he would do it in a very perverse way. He knew that she was popular and well thought of, so he couldn't openly bad-mouth her.

His strategy was to say that she was so good at what she did and was now carrying so much responsibility that she was indispensable. He would claim that to move her would be extremely detrimental to the department. Somehow, he always managed to convince the executive management that Meg should be neither promoted nor moved sideways out of Monty's reach, something she had tried on a number of occasions to achieve.

On this particular morning she walked into her department to find people huddled around a certain young woman who was crying. "What's going on?" asked Meg.

"Mr. Fisk really chewed her out in a very nasty way over something that was not her fault and has threatened to put her on performance probation," replied one of Meg's team members. "That man is a pig!"

As Meg garnered as much detail as she could about the exchange, she felt the rage building up inside.

"Why is this man making life so difficult for my staff and me?" she thought. "It's not fair and I have to put a stop to it now!"

She stormed into Monty's office. He was waiting for her, leaning way back in his chair, hands clasped behind his head and feet up on the desk, looking triumphant.

She slammed the door behind her and stood there fuming, looking at him with eyes ablaze. She was tall, slim, and very attractive, but right then she looked quite capable of killing someone — in this case, Monty Fisk.

"Why did you do that to her?" she shouted at him. "You know how she is — how easily upset she can get, and what you accused her of was not legitimate anyway, and you know it. Why do you have to be such a bully?"

He slowly took his feet off the desk, lowered his large bony hands and stood up. He was a tall, powerfully built man, and he pulled himself up to his full height. His eyes were cold and piercing. "Sit down!" he commanded in a quiet but menacing voice.

She remained standing, breathing heavily, defiant but scared. "Sit down!" he repeated, this time with a good deal more volume. She sank down into the chair. He remained standing with both hands on the desk leaning over towards her and looking down at her.

"Let me tell you something, Meg," he said quietly. "I know you think you are *Little Miss Popular* around here but I have the measure of you. You came into this company, and you advanced quickly. Do you know why?"

Not waiting for a reply, he went on. "What you don't know is that you only got your promotions because I made them happen. I saw your ability early, and I wanted to have you working for me, so I went out of my way to have you promoted. You have your job for one reason only — because of me. And I can undo what I have done if I have a mind to. I have a lot of clout in this company, Meg, because I get things done and I help them make a lot of money. I've been here a long time, and at this level what I say goes. Understand?"

Meg just sat there, saying nothing yet feeling an intense hatred for this man. He was intimidating her, but she held his gaze. There was a long pause before Monty spoke.

"You did real well for a time, and I was pleased with the way you worked. To a large extent, Meg, I still am and I wouldn't want to lose you. But you've become too damn cocky, and you constantly try to undermine my authority," continued Monty. "And I won't let you. Do you hear me? I know how you speak to the people out on the shop floor about me, and I notice how you build yourself up to be the Mother Superior around this place. I am in charge around here, Meg, not you!

"You are here to do my bidding and to do it the way I tell you to do it. I am tired of you making up your own rules and doing things any way you want. From this point on, you'd better do things the way I say they are to be done, or I might suggest to those in power some changes that you might not like. Do I make myself clear, Meg?"

"Quite clear," said Meg.

"That's good. Now get out there and get back to your job!" said Monty.

Bob

Bob Pearson was no fool. He was aware that he was slipping, and it made him very fearful. He was seeing a recurring pattern, and he didn't like it.

When an executive search firm had recruited him away from HEH, Inc., he knew it had been timely. While during the first three years of his tenure as president of that company he had produced substantial growth for it, the results had been a lot weaker during the last

The **GiCo** Story

two and were showing a pattern of steady decline. Relationships had deteriorated, and he'd begun to feel he might be losing his touch. He appeared to be sabotaging himself in many instances and was making a lot of poor decisions. He wasn't happy there.

So when the search firm had called and suggested this position at The Gyroscopic Instrument Company (GiCo), he had jumped at it. The salary was comparable, so he didn't feel demoted, plus they offered some very rich benefits. Thinking that perhaps a smaller company would better suit his management style, Bob had welcomed the opportunity.

"Happy birthday, Mr. Pearson," said Mrs. Harper in a low voice while slipping an envelope containing a very tasteful birthday card onto his desk. "Per your request, I haven't broadcast the fact of your reaching half a century — though I have to say that you don't look your age — and I don't think anyone else has remembered. You never have been one to make a fuss on your birthday, so nobody thinks much about it. Oh! Look here! Someone else does, though."

She was referring to an e-mail that had come through that morning. Bob usually checked e-mails himself during his early morning routine, but he had been so introspective on this particular day, he hadn't done so. "Somebody from your old firm. Here." She passed him the printout and quickly busied herself so as to avoid any eye contact with her boss.

The e-mail was from Rick Tanner, his old business partner from way back. Bob and Rick had started a marketing business together twenty-five years ago.

As with Bob's later ventures, all had gone well for about three years, and then things started to go south. The business almost went bankrupt, but someone decided to invest in the company and rescue it — but only on the condition that Bob leave. Rick had been the negotiator, and Bob always felt that Rick had engineered his departure.

It had been a huge blow to Bob, and for a long while he struggled to get back on his feet. But he did so eventually and found himself a good position as marketing manager of another firm that, through no fault of his own, subsequently went out of business. He then joined HEH, Inc., an engineering firm, as marketing director and subsequently, became president.

He and Rick were the same age, and although they hadn't been in contact for many years since the breakup, it was apparently the fact of it being their fiftieth that had prompted the e-mail.

Happy Birthday, Bob.
> *We've both made half a century.*
> *Congratulations are in order, I think.*
> *Call me and let's catch up.*

Rick.

Meg

Meg returned to her department seething with rage but feeling powerless. Monty had made it quite clear that he had the power to make things very difficult for her and perhaps even to get her fired. He had the authority to make that happen. Meg knew that.

By this time, the worker whom Monty had admonished was back at her station feeling sure that Meg had done all she could on her behalf to put things right with the manager.

But Meg knew different. She had made no headway at all, and she felt as though she had let the woman down. She felt like giving notice right away. "Why should I stay and be treated like dirt," she thought, "just because he feels so insecure and threatened by my efficiency and my ability to get the best out of people?"

HIDDEN AGENDAS **At Work**

This was true about Meg. She certainly had the physical bearing and presence of someone who could command respect; but she also showed a flexibility of approach that enabled the people she supervised to really trust her. This combination of strength and softness did indeed enable her to get productivity out of people in a way that Monty Fisk could never do.

But she quickly realized that leaving GiCo was out of the question. That's why she hadn't stood up to Monty. She knew she couldn't leave this company, especially now. Her husband had left her a year ago after four years of marriage, disappearing completely and leaving a lot of debt. He had become very violent and abusive, so she wasn't sorry to see him go; but there was no child support, no weekend visitations to give her a break, nothing.

She was completely on her own. Her parents were both dead, and all her brothers and sisters lived in other states. She was trapped, and she knew it.

There was another factor too that was preying on her mind. Even though she was only thirty-five, she knew that her health was not good. She'd had a couple of bouts of chronic fatigue syndrome in the past, and she was sensing that it might be returning. Lately, she was finding herself feeling very low on energy and needing more than a normal amount of sleep.

The **GiCo** Story

On the two previous occasions, she had just managed to cope well enough for people not to notice. Fortunately it had not been very severe, but to Meg, who was a single parent working at a stressful job, it had seemed debilitating. During those times she found it necessary to sleep virtually almost every hour that she wasn't working or taking care of the home and Caroline.

By doing that, she conserved enough energy to be able to effectively do her job, but by the end of the day she was truly exhausted. Each bout lasted about two months. She had researched the literature on CFS and was very aware that it can become extremely debilitating, so she knew she couldn't afford to lose her health insurance.

Meg had not had an easy life. She came from a pretty dysfunctional family. Her father was an alcoholic, and her mother was obsessive-compulsive and ultra critical. Everything had to be perfect for her, which meant that whatever Meg did was never good enough.

However hard she tried to please her mother, she could never win her approval. Meg's mother blamed her for everything, and, perhaps because Meg was the eldest child, used her as the scapegoat for all the dysfunction within the family.

Meg's father was in and out of work because of his drinking and he began molesting her when she was three years old. As it is for many girls who are molested by their fathers, she initially found it pleasurable and enjoyed getting the attention from the man she had put on a pedestal and from whom she got no attention at all except in that way.

At the same time, however, the deep knowing that it was wrong and shouldn't be happening would well up inside her and induce terrible guilt and fear. The longer the molestation went on, the worse Meg's feelings became. She was extremely frightened of him, and although she wanted the abuse to stop, she was powerless to do anything about it.

She did what most abuse victims do in this situation: she split herself off and disassociated from what was happening and then repressed the pain. When she was twelve, she tried to tell her mother about the abuse but her mother only became extremely enraged about it and would not listen. She just denied it and then shamed Meg even more for suggesting such a thing. Meg felt totally trapped and abandoned.

Finally, at age sixteen, Meg left home. She basically ran away without telling her parents where she was going, which was no big deal since they were too out of it to care anyway. For the next few years she became very promiscuous and totally irresponsible. She tried being in a lesbian relationship for a while, but that didn't work out.

The **GiCo** Story

At age twenty-four she was badly beaten and raped by a man she met in a bar one night. That incident put her into the hospital for three days, but fortunately, she recognized it as her wake-up call. She decided then to give up drinking and drugs and to really pull her life together. She moved, got a decent job, and began building her life again.

She got married at twenty-five to a man who had seemed decent enough at first, but who very soon became violent and emotionally abusive. He drank heavily, and Meg often feared for her life when he would come home drunk.

Her daughter Caroline was from this marriage, but there was doubt about who the father was because Meg had had a short but passionate affair with another man. Her husband never suspected, but Meg became fearful for Caroline's safety as well as her own, so she eventually left that marriage and was divorced at twenty-eight.

She did well on her own for a while but she was lonely and in need of support. The chronic fatigue happened during this time, and it scared her to think that she might not be able to support herself and Caroline. She got married again, mostly for that reason, this time to a man who wasn't exactly abusive but who became emotionally unavailable very soon after the wedding.

It was a relationship without passion or interest. It was just dull. Meg wasn't the sort of woman to put up with that so she left him. At thirty-four she found herself alone once more.

Having come out of two failed marriages, Meg pretty much made up her mind that she wasn't going to marry, or even live with a man again, at least not until Caroline was grown up and gone. "All men are selfish and irresponsible," she would say. "They just use you and dump you, and I just don't want anything to do with any of them! I'm fine on my own."

In the year since she had become divorced, she had indeed done pretty well on her own. She had more or less gotten herself out of debt and managed to keep the mortgage paid, keep a car, and take care of herself and Caroline. She had progressed in the company and was earning a decent wage. It seemed that the only fly in the ointment was Monty. "Why does he have to make things so difficult for me?" she wondered.

As she sat there in her office thinking about it and still fuming, she wondered aloud how she could get back at him. "Get him fired perhaps? Now wouldn't that be good? Well, no. Can't do that. But I'll make sure he gets no cooperation from me in the future. I'm tired of working hard and making him look good."

The bell indicating that it was time for her department to take a coffee break shook her out of her obsessive thinking about how to get back at Monty. "Gotta get on with the job," she told herself. "But let me get a good strong cup of coffee first!"

Bob

The e-mail had unsettled Bob even more than he already had been before Mrs. Harper had handed it to him. "Why would he write after all these years? Our relationship ended so acrimoniously."

Mrs. Harper was still in earshot but he was really talking to himself. She chose not to respond. Bob felt some pain in the area of his heart and knew it instinctively to be a reminder of the pain of being in that relationship — the pain that he had largely suppressed.

Right from the start Rick had made him feel "less than." No matter how hard he worked or how much effort he put in, it was never enough. Rick found fault with everything he did. Even though they were, in fact, equal partners, Rick had always acted as if he were the boss, and had treated Bob accordingly, often making decisions unilaterally.

HIDDEN AGENDAS **At Work**

Where Bob was cautious and conservative, Rick was a risk taker. It was this quality that had gotten the company into financial trouble and headed towards bankruptcy. He managed to twist everything around and made it look as if it were all Bob's fault, pointing to Bob's "weak management style" as the cause of the failure. Rick succeeded to the extent that the investors who came in to rescue the company agreed with him and made it a condition of the bailout that Bob had to go.

It had been a huge betrayal for Bob. It hadn't helped Bob's self esteem either to learn that, after he left, the company leaped ahead and then years later went public. Rick virtually retired a multimillionaire at age forty-two.

Bob looked again at the e-mail and decided not to take Rick up on the suggestion that they reconnect. The memory of it all was just too much. He crumpled the e-mail very tightly into a ball and tossed it into the trash can. The pain in his chest did not go away.

Mrs. Harper noticed the pained expression on Bob's face but decided to say nothing nor even to let him know that she noticed. She had been working for him for the entire time he had been at the company but had recently found herself having to tiptoe around him all the time, making sure not to get him upset. The president of the company was clearly not himself.

Monty

Monty was fuming and breathing heavily. It took him quite some time to compose himself after Meg turned her back and walked out of his office, slamming the door hard as she left.

There was something about Meg he just couldn't abide. It seemed that hardly a day passed by where she didn't find some way to get under his skin. Everything she did seemed to upset him — and often to a disproportionate extent. He frequently had to admit that to himself.

He also had to concede that she was a good worker who did her job well — there was no doubt about that. The workers adored and respected her because she was both firm and fair. They didn't mess with her, but whenever the need arose, she stood up for them — oftentimes against him. That really angered him.

When she had first joined the company and begun working for him, he had been very comfortable with her. He found her to be teachable and responsive, intelligent and willing to grow into the job. He had liked Meg in the beginning and had vigorously supported her promotion to production supervisor. But as she came into her power and began to exercise more and more responsibility, Monty's feelings began to change. He

HIDDEN AGENDAS **At Work**

felt threatened by her. He began to feel that she was undermining him at every opportunity and setting the workers against him. He felt defensive around her, and although she always treated him with due respect, he felt dominated by her in some strange way. She seemed so overpowering!

Monty sat there at his desk, going over what had just happened, feeling puzzled and perplexed. He never thought of himself as an angry man. So why so much anger? What was it about Meg that upset him so much? He couldn't figure it out at all, other than to assume it was some kind of personality clash. He had to admit that he had chewed that worker out on purpose, knowing that Meg would rise to the bait and come in with guns ablaze, giving him the opportunity to put her down. But he still couldn't quite understand why he needed to do it.

Whatever the reason, Monty resolved to stay on top of her and not let her get the better of him. She had so much support from the workers that she could easily usurp his authority and become, in effect, the boss. He must not allow that to happen.

"I need to clip her wings," he said to himself, thinking that it wasn't beyond the bounds of possibility that Meg might threaten his position in the company by causing labor disputes over his leadership style.

The **GiCo** Story

"That won't happen," he said as if to comfort himself. "Bob Pearson will support me over her any day." With that he returned to work.

There did, in fact, exist an unusually close bond between the president and his production manager, such that Monty had every reason to feel more secure in his job than he otherwise might. They had met when they both worked at the company Bob joined after being ejected from his own company by Rick. Bob was a few years older than Monty but saw a great deal of potential in him. Monty was talented, sharp and had a natural flair for organization and production.

While Bob had actually been on the sales and marketing side of that business, he really felt a greater affinity to the manufacturing and production side. In that sense, he was a square peg in a round hole. That being so, he began to derive a vicarious satisfaction from mentoring Monty. Bob used what influence he had at the time to make sure that Monty had ample opportunity to grow in the company during the five years Bob was there.

When Monty eventually applied for and landed another job, Bob felt not only disappointment but a strong sense of betrayal. Monty had not even mentioned he was looking for another position. Bob knew his feelings were irrational and that he had no right to expect Monty to stay. Nothing was ever said, but Monty felt Bob's disappointment and anger.

HIDDEN AGENDAS **At Work**

He did stay in touch with Bob, if only sporadically and mostly by e-mail. Usually it was just to share some success at work, a promotion perhaps and the contact occurred no more than a couple of times a year.

However, when Monty heard that the president of the company where he worked, GiCo, Inc., was retiring and that the likelihood was that either one of two people he despised equally in the company were likely to take his place, he immediately thought of his old mentor, Bob Pearson, who was at that time president of HEH, Inc.

Having Bob at the helm of the company where he worked would secure his own position nicely, Monty had reasoned. Monty would do anything to stop Dennis Barker from becoming president. He'd frequently had run-ins with Dennis and knew that if Dennis became president, life might become very precarious.

Dennis Barker was always bitching about how the production department did not keep the sales force properly supported, but as far as Monty was concerned it was Dennis Barker's inefficiency and inability to plan ahead that caused the problems. Dennis treated him with disdain, and Monty could barely bring himself to talk with Dennis.

Monty had dashed off an e-mail letting Bob know that a search firm had been given the task of finding a new

The **GiCo** Story

president for GiCo. He gave Bob a contact number he had somehow acquired and left it at that. Bob took the bait, and the rest was history.

The debt had only once been acknowledged and, even then, well before Bob took the helm at GiCo. From the moment Bob arrived at the firm, Monty had been assiduous in maintaining a careful and respectful distance and had never tried to curry favor with Bob. Neither had Bob resumed his mentoring role, and he treated Monty just like any of his other managers.

However, Monty always knew that he had an ace in the hole and that, one day, he might need to make use of it. It gave him a lot of comfort.

Dennis

Whenever Dennis Barker entered the room, it was like someone had opened the door and allowed a gust of wind to blow in and completely occupy the space. His energy was enormous, and he got your attention immediately, and yet there was always something inauthentic about him. One never could feel quite comfortable with him. He was always too eager to please and generous to a fault; people always felt there was another agenda behind everything Dennis said and did. "I've got the figures, Bob," he said as he blew into the room.

HIDDEN AGENDAS **At Work**

"How do they look?" asked Bob with a sinking feeling. He knew they weren't going to be good.

"Not so great," replied Dennis. "We need to talk. Is this a good time? I can come back later if you like."

Bob motioned with his hand for Dennis to sit and held out his hand for the most recent sales figures that Dennis had just prepared. Dennis sat down and drew his chair up closer to Bob's desk. "Oh, and by the way, happy birthday," he said.

Bob peered over his spectacles at Dennis and just grunted, nodding in reluctant acknowledgment. He felt anything but happy. Dennis cast a glance back and gave a shrug as if to say, "Well, I tried."

He knew Bob was depressed and struggling to stay together for some reason. Dennis had no idea what was eating Bob but surmised that he and Jean might be having troubles at home. She seemed nice enough, but she liked all the trappings and was always out spending Bob's money at all the finest stores. Perhaps she had gotten him into serious debt. Dennis doubted it though. It seemed Bob was troubled more by what was inside him than by any external circumstances.

Dennis had been watching Bob like a hawk over the last six months and was very aware that Bob was not himself and might even be losing his grip. This might be his chance to replace Bob, he allowed himself to think, but he would need to play his cards very carefully.

"This is just a temporary dip in the figures, Bob," Dennis said reassuringly. "They'll pick up next quarter for sure. We had so many things not going for us this quarter that will not be factored in next time around. The sales team is much stronger now, and we have built in some good incentives to improve performance."

"With the economy the way it is, we ought to be performing better than this, though," replied Bob as he looked over the figures.

"Bob, you must give yourself credit. Under your leadership, we doubled our net income for each of the first three years of your tenure. That was a tremendous achievement, and I have no doubt in my mind that no one else could have done it *(unspoken subtext: except me, of course).* I agree it has slowed down somewhat, but it is still good and we are still growing. However, and I hate to say this Bob, but if we have a problem at all, it is not with sales and marketing but with production."

Bob bristled. Manufacturing and production were his responsibility, and here was Dennis interfering again in his usual manner. He always came on first with the

HIDDEN AGENDAS **At Work**

compliments and then hit you from behind with the criticism. Bob immediately snapped back at Dennis, "What are you saying?"

Dennis knew he was on dangerous ground and would have to tread carefully, but he had seen an opportunity. "We need to modernize our systems, Bob. Our costs are much higher than our competitors', and yet we still have to compete on price and service. The sales people are very frustrated because we are consistently unable to supply the product in a timely fashion and they lose sales as a result of that."

"I'm ahead of you on this, Dennis," replied Bob. "I have already asked Monty Fisk to submit ideas for modernizing the plant."

Dennis leaned forward in his seat, not looking at Bob but at his own feet with his hands tightly clasped together between his legs. He knew how to use his energy to create presence. Pausing for quite some time, he finally looked at Bob and said, "But Monty Fisk is the problem, Bob."

"What the hell do you mean?" Bob responded angrily. "Monty Fisk is a hell of a good production manager."

In his spare time Dennis was a fly fisherman and a good one at that. Now he felt almost as if he were

The **GiCo** Story

playing Bob like a fish on a line. Bob had taken the bait and now Dennis had to carefully reel him in.

Though Bob didn't realize it, Dennis knew only too well that Monty Fisk had tipped him off about the opening for president and was, in that sense, at least partly responsible for Dennis not getting the job. He hated Fisk, so there was a score to settle there too — but of course Bob, or rather his job, was the bigger fish. He was using a 'minnow to catch a mackerel,' as they say, and it would be sweet revenge indeed if he could dispose of them both at the same time.

Not only did he know of their connection and the debt that Bob owed Monty, but in doing his homework well, Dennis had discovered that Bob had been Monty's mentor for some years prior. That added another whole dimension to the situation and further ammunition.

"He's of the old school, Bob," replied Dennis softly. "He won't modernize — he's too stuck in his ways. He doesn't understand computers and is unable to hold a vision big enough to spearhead the kind of improvements needed to support the kind of growth we need to have if we want to keep our market share. Our competitors are way ahead of us in terms of efficiency and profitability, Bob, and you know it. We've been putting off the modernizing plan for some time now, to the point where some drastic action is required."

HIDDEN AGENDAS **At Work**

"You might be surprised!" Bob countered. "He'll be reporting to me with his suggestions for modernization by the end of this month. As soon as we have them, we'll have a meeting to discuss them. Until then, the subject is closed! Now, if there's nothing else, Dennis, I need to get back to work."

Clearly, the meeting was at an end, but Dennis felt pleased with the limited outcome of this exchange and, with all due deference, gracefully made his exit.

Dennis was a patient man but he was also driven. He wanted Bob's job so much he could taste it. He had watched Bob build the company fast in his first three years but was now recognizing the signs that Bob was weakening. His patience and stealth were starting to pay off, and he was about to turn up the heat.

Over the past twelve months, Dennis had carefully sown seeds of discontent about Bob among the management team. This had trickled down to the shop floor and to the sales team. As a result, people were now beginning to question Bob's ability as president.

Using divide-and-rule tactics, Dennis nurtured the discontent between sales and marketing and the production departments, and put the squeeze on Monty Fisk so he would feel vulnerable. Dennis knew that in order to survive, Monty would play his ace card on Bob, which would create enormous embarrassment

The **GiCo** Story

for Bob and perhaps even a crisis. That was exactly what Dennis wanted.

BOB

Though he had escaped birthday celebrations at work, Bob was not to be let off so lightly at home. Jean had arranged a surprise birthday party for him. He arrived home earlier than usual and found that she had invited several friends to be there, as well as his now quite aged father.

As he walked through the door they all sang "Happy Birthday," and his children rushed up to him to give him their gifts. Jean kissed him lovingly.

She was younger than Bob by eight years and was an attractive, stylish woman with shoulder-length, ash-blonde hair which she usually wore down, but on this occasion she had put it up. She wore a low-cut, tight fitting white dress that revealed quite of lot of her shapely figure. Bob did his best to look pleased about the party and, once things settled down a bit, proceeded to pour champagne for a toast.

"To my loving husband on his fiftieth birthday," said Jean simply. Everyone clapped and cheered.

HIDDEN AGENDAS At Work

"Thanks, everyone: let's eat," Bob said, pointing to the lavish buffet that Jean had had catered. Once he had filled his plate, Bob reluctantly made his way over to his father.

In spite of having lost a leg in the Second World War and then later becoming crippled through a car accident when Bob was just a baby, Bob's father had reached the age of seventy-nine. Though confined to a wheelchair for most of his life, he had managed to outlive Bob's mother by fifteen years. He was an extremely angry and bitter man.

"Hi, Dad. How are you doing?" Bob asked dutifully.

"Terrible!" came the reply that Bob had fully expected. "The pain gets worse every year, and those stupid doctors at the VA Hospital couldn't give a damn. Not one of them! Useless bastards, all of 'em. But I don't give in, and I still work my ass off in spite of the pain. I don't quit you know; not like some people I know."

There was the first jab of the evening that Bob knew was inevitable and inescapable. There would be more.

"And how about you? Still at that company — what's it called?"

"GiCo, Dad."

The **GiCo** Story

"Yes, that's it, GiCo. Heard from that old partner of yours lately, the one who became a millionaire? You screwed up there, didn't you, boy? Shouldn't have left. You might have been a millionaire by now too."

"I didn't exactly leave, Dad, and I'm not doing so bad anyway. Does this make me look poor?" asked Bob, pointing to the house and everything in it.

"No, but you're not a millionaire either, are you? That partner of yours is a multimillionaire, though, isn't he? Let's face it, Bobby, you both started out together as partners and you let him screw you over. Pity you're not more like your brother. Jimmy wouldn't have let that bastard squeeze him out. No siree! If it had been him and not you, I wouldn't have lost the money I put into that business to help you get going. Hard-earned cash — made by my own hands, let me tell you, even though I am in a damned wheelchair. I ended up losing my money because of you."

"Must you bring that up again, Dad? You know darn well I repaid that debt years ago."

"Yeah, so I got my money back, but I might have been a millionaire when Rick took that company public if you hadn't screwed up, just like I knew you would. Instead, I have to rely on my pension and whatever I make by selling my woodworking."

HIDDEN AGENDAS **At Work**

"Fuck you, Dad!" said Bob and moved away. He could feel the rage welling up in him, and he was close to tears. He hated the man and wished that Jean had not invited him. Even though his mother had not been emotionally available for him during his early years, he nevertheless missed her and wished all the time that it was his father that had died of cancer instead.

When Bob was a young boy, his father would always put him down and would frequently belittle him in front of people. "Look at him," he would shout and scream. "He'll never amount to anything; no damn use to anyone! Thank God his brother Jimmy isn't like him!"

As is typical with this kind of primal wounding, and in spite of all the shaming and the beatings that inevitably followed, Bob had unconsciously spent all his boyhood and most of his adult life trying to get his father's approval and never succeeding.

Every time Bob had experienced failure in his life, his thoughts would go straight to his father and the shame would be unbearable. Conversely, whenever he achieved success, no matter how good it was, he knew it would never be enough.

As a boy, Bob was athletic, wiry and strong. He was not one for team sports, but he was a good long-distance runner. He ran in a lot of races and won a fair number of trophies. His father never came to watch or support him, except once. That was when Bob was fourteen and was representing his high school in a ten-mile cross-country race. Bob came in first but only a few yards in front of the next contender. The only comment his father made was, "You nearly lost!"

The only person Bob had felt really loved him and made him feel worthwhile was his grandfather. He lived close by, and from a very early age, Bob spent as many hours with him as he could. Bob's mother and father took no notice of him anyway, so they didn't care. His grandfather had a little workshop and would show Bob how to do things with bits of wood and metal. With him, Bob did not feel alone.

Though he visited his grandfather most days, there was one day that Bob, for whatever reason, decided not to. That was the day his grandfather died. The neighbors had found him in his workshop, having died alone of a massive heart attack.

Bob was just five years of age, but it felt to him as if his whole world had come crashing down. He had lost the only person in the world that loved him and saw him for who he was. He had never felt so desperately alone, and yet, he could share none of his pain with his parents, least of all his father. His father had just told him not be so stupid. "Cryin' is for girls," he said and told Bob to stop crying or he would give him something to cry about.

HIDDEN AGENDAS **At Work**

Bob also blamed himself for the death. "If only I had gone there as usual, I might have been able to save him — or at least call an ambulance," he would always think to himself. Bob never got over the loss.

Fortunately, the guests left pretty early and, thank God, someone helped Bob's father get himself into the wheelchair-adapted mini-van that he drove. Bob had said nothing more to him the whole evening and was glad to see him go. He did not even say good-bye, and neither did his father.

"The mean old bastard," he said quietly to Jean as they watched him go. "I'll hate him until the day he dies, and then some."

"I'm sorry I invited him, Bob, but it felt right somehow that I should. It's been so long since you two have spoken, and after all, it is your fiftieth. But I know now that I shouldn't have. I'm sorry."

Bob turned and looked at his wife. She looked alluring in her low-cut dress, and whereas normally he would have been quick to seize the moment, he felt no desire for her tonight. "I've got to go to bed," he said. "I am so desperately tired." With that, and with his head held low, he went upstairs.

Jean knew him well enough to know that something was desperately wrong, so for the first time in her life she left the house just as it was and immediately followed him upstairs to bed. She knew that he needed her.

Bob ended his fiftieth birthday in the arms of his wife, crying uncontrollably for most of the night. And he didn't know why.

Meg

Meg couldn't get Monty off her mind. He had scared her that day — much more than she realized at the time. She really felt that he had it in for her, even though she did her job more or less perfectly.

She was a perfectionist about everything, but with Monty it counted for nothing. Whatever she did, it was not enough for him. Thank God that the workers cared for her and that she was able to put her energy into taking care of them.

Meg collected Caroline from school and went straight home. Immediately after cooking them both a light meal, she crashed.

Mrs. Harper

Gwen Harper was one of those women who you might think had been born with energy-sensing antennae. She could not only register emotional tension between people three blocks away but would have a pretty good sense of what it might be about. Not that she was psychic. The kind of sensitivity she had came from being brought up in a house where one or both parents are not only alcoholic but violent rage-a-holics as well.

To survive and to stay out of trouble for as long as possible, Gwen had had to develop an ultra sensitive awareness of where the next emotional outburst might come from and to recognize the warning signs instantly. She also learned to say very little or, better still, to say nothing about what she saw or heard going on around her. The safest strategy was to act as if nothing had happened and be as invisible as possible.

She continued to effect that strategy at GiCo, much as she had likely done in her own marriage. Her husband had died ten years ago, and her four children were all grown and married. She lived alone with her two cats.

Gwen was fully aware of all the ongoing tensions between Bob Pearson and Dennis Barker, and she saw through all the subtle and not-so-subtle power plays in which each of them indulged. But they didn't know that, of course. She had perfected the art of being invisible and giving the impression of being totally unaware of what was happening around her. She never spoke of what she observed and never offered advice. She had strong opinions, of course, but she always kept them to herself.

She also knew a lot about Bob Pearson's background by virtue of the fact that her old school friend, Barbara Fields, had ended up marrying Rick Tanner. Gwen had maintained that connection and had therefore, through Barbara, heard all about the drama that occurred when Rick forced Bob Pearson out of their partnership.

Naturally, she saw it all through Barbara Tanner's eyes at the time and never did meet Bob. Neither had she ever let on to Bob when he joined the firm that she was an acquaintance of the Tanners or that she knew what had happened. She almost lost it, though, when that e-mail came in from Rick on Bob's birthday. She came close to letting out a gasp when she saw it, but Bob was too self-absorbed to notice.

Her awareness of what was going on was not limited to the executive floor. She somehow managed to stay in tune with the emotional energy field of the entire firm. She had a good ear for the gossip that is common between secretaries and assistants, and she was

HIDDEN AGENDAS At Work

able to make correct intuitive connections with only the smallest tidbits of information. She was also able to confirm her intuitions by going to the personnel files to which, as the president's personal assistant, she had unfettered access.

Gwen came from a large family. She was the second of six children: four boys and two girls. Her older brother, 3 years her senior, treated her just like her father treated her mother. Her father was of the firm opinion that women didn't matter much and didn't require a higher education because they would become either a nurse, a schoolteacher, or a secretary.

When her father sold his business for 14.4 million dollars, the boys got equal shares; the two girls got nothing. Not a penny. Gwen was furious but could never confront her father. He was just too powerful, and she was terrified of him.

Her mother was a kind and sweet soul with a weak body. She was always sick in bed or moving around feeling terrible. It saddened Gwen to see her father be so demanding of her mother in spite of the fact that she was weak, exhausted and ill. It was as if he didn't even notice.

In order to protect her mother, Gwen began to work around the house at a very early age and to take care of the other children. Her only sister was the baby in

The **GiCo** Story

the family, so basically Gwen became mother and maid in that household. The boys were not expected to help out in the house in any way, and her father expected to be looked after all the time.

Her early life was a real struggle, and when she got pregnant in her late teens, her father disowned her, saying she brought shame on the family even though she married the man prior to the child being born.

She despised Monty Fisk. She knew of his prior connection with Bob, of course, and understood only too well how he had set it up with the search firm to recruit Bob Pearson in order to sabotage Dennis Barker's chances of becoming president.

Not that Gwen Harper had much time for Dennis Barker either, let it be said, but she had been extremely attached and loyal to Charles Bottomly, the other candidate, who had died within a year of retiring. She really had wanted him to get the job, and she firmly believed that he would be alive today had he done so. In her mind, it was the disappointment that had killed him, and to a large extent, she blamed Monty Fisk.

It was also not escaping her keen attention that Dennis Barker was maneuvering himself to wrest back from Bob Pearson the job that Dennis had always felt was his, by aggravating and capitalizing upon Bob's current state of depression. She could read Dennis like a book.

HIDDEN AGENDAS At Work

Though she had been loyal to Charles Bottomly and was disappointed that Bob Pearson was appointed, she nevertheless liked Bob from the beginning. She very soon became willing to defend and protect him from all the covert negative energy that was projected towards him, and she wasn't going to stop now.

Neither was she going to let Dennis Barker hurt Bob. She was an extremely good and loyal secretary to Bob, but she was sensitive to his feelings too and worried about him when he felt down. It was all she could do not to mother him.

Besides having this uncanny ability to know everything that was going on without appearing to do so, and to remain more or less invisible, she also had a very strong caretaker streak. If she saw someone being treated unfairly in any way, she would feel their pain intensely and would work in very subtle ways to make sure that some restitution occurred.

In her mind, she saw the people who worked at GiCo as her family, and she felt a deep need to be responsible for them, just as she had been with her own siblings.

This need to be a "silent" caretaker and anonymous benefactor fitted in with her need to be invisible and to keep everything she knew inside and hidden. However, it led her to exist very much in her own inner world, separate from other people. Though on the surface she was quite sociable, no one could get close to her.

The shadow side of Gwen Harper's ability to "take care" of people without drawing attention to herself was that she was equally adept at secretly sabotaging those she didn't like and about whom she had strong judgments. She was very self-righteous and was always quite sure she knew what was best.

Her current concern, however, was with Meg Smith. She really liked Meg and felt very drawn to her, seeing a lot of herself in her perhaps. She had heard a lot about Meg and her wilder days but had developed a lot of respect for how Meg had pulled herself up by her bootstraps and made a decent life for herself when she might easily have gone the other way. Not that Gwen was above taking some credit for this herself. After all, it was she who had pulled a lot of strings to get Meg her job at GiCo.

It was during her abusive first marriage that Meg had met Rick Tanner and had a brief affair with him. His wife Barbara never knew about it, so Gwen, too, would have remained ignorant of that had Rick not called and asked if she could get Meg a job at GiCo.

He had said that she was a friend and just wanted to do her a favor, but Gwen could smell the guilt and the de-

HIDDEN AGENDAS **At Work**

ception. She knew what a womanizer Rick was and knew immediately that he had, or was having, an affair with Meg. When Meg arrived at the interview, she was clearly pregnant, and even though Meg was married, Gwen had no doubt whatsoever in her own mind that the baby was Rick's.

At the time she was very angry with Meg for having the affair with her friend's husband and judged her severely, but she knew Rick well enough to know that it would have been mostly his fault. As time went by, she dropped her judgment and began to really like Meg. She saw a lot of herself there.

She recognized Meg as being a good mother to Caroline and a very good supervisor at work. She particularly appreciated the way that she took good care of her workers and was willing to defend them against that horrible tyrant and woman-hater, Monty Fisk.

She had been carefully tracking how Monty had turned on Meg and blocked her promotion on a number of occasions. Gwen had listened to Monty telling Bob Pearson how Meg needed strong handling and that she might be trouble if Bob moved her into another department and gave her a promotion. Bob always gave in to Monty, and Gwen Harper knew why, of course — which is why she decided that she would intervene as soon as the opportunity presented itself.

BOB

Gwen Harper took the call. "Mrs. Harper, this is Jean Pearson. Would you please tell everyone who needs to know that Mr. Pearson will not be in today? I think he might have picked up a bit of food poisoning at the party we threw for him last night — not real serious, I don't think — so he should be in tomorrow. Would you do that for me? Thanks. Bye."

Bob threw a glance at Jean and wondered whether he would indeed be able to pull himself together sufficiently to return to work in the morning. He had never called in sick in his life, and for him to take a day off was quite unusual and totally out of character. *(That fact had not been lost on Mrs. Harper, either.)* He looked, and felt, terrible.

Jean had gotten the kids off to school, and now they were alone. She had been worried about him for months, but he would never talk about his feelings and always brushed her aside whenever she asked him if he was worried about anything.

"What's going on, Bob?" she asked. "You've never cried like that for as long as I've known you. You were like a scared little boy last night in bed. You need to talk about it, Bob, or you'll crack up."

HIDDEN AGENDAS **At Work**

Bob just stared vacantly into the fireplace. He would not look at Jean. Finally he said, "I'm scared of losing it all, Jean. I feel that I am in quicksand, and I am being sucked down."

"By what, Bob?" Jean asked.

"I don't know."

"Are things getting really difficult at work again? Is that it? Is Dennis putting pressure on you?" Jean waited for a response that was long in coming.

"Yes, but that's not it. I've had work troubles like this before, and I can handle Dennis Barker. I know he wants my job, but I'm always one step ahead of him." "Then what is it, Bob? Is it us?"

"No," said Bob quickly, looking up at her. "It's not our relationship. I love you, and we're fine."

Jean had run out of questions and could only look at him and observe how pathetic and childlike he seemed at this moment.

"I feel like I am dying," he said.

"What do you mean?" Jean cried.

"Oh, don't panic — it's not my health. I'm fine physically. No, I'm not going to die — I'm just saying that this feels like death to me."

With that, Bob buried his head in his hands and then, after a few moments, got up and hurried to their bedroom. She knew he needed to cry alone.

Dennis

After Gwen Harper had called and told him that Bob Pearson was sick and wouldn't be in, Dennis allowed himself a wry smile. He knew that Bob was close to a breakdown and sensed that this might be his best opportunity yet to oust Bob and take over his job.
From an early age, Dennis had been driven to be number one. In his eyes, coming second was the same as losing, so winning was everything to him. With that kind of mindset, the ends always justified the means, and Dennis had followed that path all his life. So long as he won in the end, he had no qualms about how he did it.

But he was as smart a man as he was ruthless. He was extremely patient, knowing how to bide his time and wait for the right moment to strike. He also had

HIDDEN AGENDAS At Work

perfected the art of the act and always gave the impression of being everything that he was not.

He had studied and mastered Neuro-Linguistic Programming (NLP). This is a form of awake-hypnosis that was originally designed as a powerful healing modality for reprogramming the subconscious mind. However, because it was a form of hypnosis that was performed while the person was totally conscious, it could also be performed surreptitiously.

This made NLP very attractive to people who wanted to manipulate others at the subconscious level without their being aware of it. Salesmen, obviously, thought of it as a blessing and Dennis was no exception. He became extremely adept at using it to control others. It was largely through his ability to control and manipulate people without their knowing, and to be how he thought others wanted him to be, that he advanced his career in sales in general and at GiCo in particular.

Dennis was born into a family of Irish descent. Both sets of grandparents had immigrated during the potato famine of 1910 and had settled in Boston. Dennis' parents were very poor and his father was a drinker. Dennis was the fifth child of eight and always felt that he had to fight for mere survival. He had always felt deeply ashamed of his family and vowed that he wasn't going to end up like his father, a broken man. Out of

The **GiCo** Story

all the children, he was the one who took himself off to night school with the sole aim of lifting himself out of the lifestyle he despised and to escape the family he was so terribly ashamed of. He was intelligent and a fast learner.

He had succeeded in becoming a well-educated engineer, but he soon was drawn towards the sales side of the business. His Irish charm and a gift for quick thinking and fast talking made him a natural for sales. He had joined GiCo, Inc., some ten years previously as a technical salesman and had steadily risen through the ranks to become vice president at the age of thirty-six.

From very early on, Dennis had set his sights on the top job and was extremely disappointed and angry when he didn't get it. Not that he showed it, of course. That wasn't his style. He appeared to take it in his stride and to support the board's choice, but inside he was seething. He vowed that he would do whatever he had to do to wrest that job, at the earliest opportunity, from whomever held it at the time. Dennis would not be happy until he was number one at GiCo, Inc.

But he was never one to attack directly. Dennis knew that if he was too overt in trying to unseat the president, that Bob would fight him very hard and might well fire him.

HIDDEN AGENDAS **At Work**

No, he knew that the best way to get Bob Pearson was through Monty Fisk. With Bob away at least for a day and probably more than that, this was a good time to sow some seeds and to begin unsettling Monty to the point where Monty might feel it necessary to play his survival card with Bob Pearson. Dennis picked up the phone and asked his secretary to put a call through to Monty Fisk.

Gwen Harper

Gwen Harper was also sharp enough to see an opportunity when it presented itself. She put a call through to one of the secretarial staff in the production department she trusted well enough to know that it wouldn't get to Monty Fisk's personal secretary, to the effect that Mrs. Harper would like to have a word with Meg Smith. A few minutes later, her phone rang.

"Hello, Mrs. Harper, this is Meg Smith from production. I was told that you wanted to speak with me."

"That's right, Meg," Gwen replied. "I would like a word with you if you have a moment. Actually, I would prefer that it be off the premises. Would you care to have lunch with me today?"

"Of course," said Meg. "That would be nice. I get my lunch break around one o'clock. Is that OK?"

Gwen told Meg to meet her at 1:15 at a particular restaurant and to not let anyone, especially Mr. Fisk, know that she was having lunch with Gwen Harper. Meg arrived on time, and as soon as they had ordered, Gwen opened the conversation.

"Meg, I've been noticing that you haven't been yourself lately. You look very tired and stressed out. I'm worried about you. What's going on?"

"Oh, nothing really," Meg replied, a little taken aback by Gwen's directness. She had been wondering all morning why Gwen had quite uncharacteristically suggested a lunchtime meeting. "I'm just a little tired trying to be a mom as well as a full-time career woman. But I'm fine, really."

"Is Mr. Fisk still coming down hard on you?" asked Gwen, thinking that she had to come to the point quickly. "I'm hearing on the grapevine that he is making things really tough for you. Is that right?"

Tears immediately began coming to Meg's eyes. She could feel Gwen's concern for her and immediately connected with her compassion. Even though she was an executive secretary, Gwen could just as easily be your mother in moments like this.

HIDDEN AGENDAS **At Work**

Meg dropped her guard and began to relate to Gwen all that had been going on between her and Monty and how it was wearing her down and undermining her self-esteem. She told Gwen how Monty had threatened her the day before and how he had wielded his power over her. She just couldn't understand why he hated her so much, especially since in the early days he had seemed to like her and had supported her.

For her part, Gwen was acutely aware that her own dislike for Monty Fisk and her desire to protect Meg from his overbearing behavior were becoming even more intense.

"Please don't say anything to Mr. Pearson, Mrs. Harper," Meg pleaded. "If this gets back to Monty, my life won't be worth living."

"Don't worry, Meg. I won't. But I won't let Monty get away with anything either. If he threatens you again, I want you to let me know. I cannot stand injustice, and even more so, I hate the idea of men trying to use their strength to overpower women. I won't let it happen to you, Meg." Meg felt relieved and cared for. It was a good feeling.

When Gwen Harper got back to the office, she checked messages and found none from the Pearsons. She thought it was strange, but took advantage of the time and the freedom to go into the personnel files. She

The **GiCo** Story

was hoping she could find something on Monty Fisk that would weaken his hold over Bob Pearson.

She was in something of a quandary though, because she sensed that Dennis was also getting ready to pounce on Monty Fisk for reasons of his own. She knew he knew about Bob and Monty and had been waiting for an opportunity to expose the whole situation in order to embarrass Bob, so she was not anxious to provide him with any ammunition. Dennis could care less about Meg Smith.

Gwen thought long and hard and then made a fateful decision that would ultimately change the fortunes of GiCo, Inc. She called Rick Tanner and told him about Bob.

Bob

Bob slept virtually all that day, all through the night and into the next morning. Jean was happy about that. She knew that nothing heals like an extended sleep, and she left him alone as much as she could, except to bring him water and some snack food which he hardly touched. She saw it as the direct result of stress and feared that it might have been a nervous breakdown. It did not, however, occur to her that it might be his dark night of the soul.

Bob, on the other hand, had a sense of it being just that, though he would never have used that language to describe it. Yes, stress was a factor, but what was happening to him was caused by something far more profound. Some part of himself was boiling up and wanting to surface, but he didn't understand what it was or how he should react. Bob was scared.

About mid-morning a FedEx packet arrived. Jean looked at it but didn't open it before taking it up to Bob, who was now sitting up and feeling a little better. He opened it and found that it contained a book. He looked to see who had sent it, but it had been dispatched by a bookstore addressed to Mr. Robert Pearson. There was no note, no invoice, nothing.

The title of the book intrigued him: *Radical Forgiveness: Making Room for the Miracle*. He had never heard of the author nor even any of those who had endorsed the book. Shrugging his shoulders, he put it down on his bedside cabinet and went back to sleep.

Once more, Jean left him alone but kept on wondering who had sent Bob that book — and why that one? Not that he didn't need a miracle right now! "He could really use one," she thought.

After lunch that day, she decided she must talk with Dennis Barker and Gwen Harper and give them some idea when Bob might be returning. She didn't want to

The **GiCo** Story

say too much, but there was no hiding that something quite serious was happening.

She told them that Bob was suffering from nervous exhaustion and that she thought he needed to take at least a week off, if not two. On the other hand, he would probably be available for consultation from home in the next day or two.

She only talked to Mrs. Harper, but she knew that the message would get to everyone who needed to know. She went back up to Bob about two hours later just to check on him and found him sitting up and almost devouring the book. He seemed to have gotten some of his life back all of a sudden.

"Jean, whoever sent this book must have known something. It's really quite extraordinary, and even though it's not my normal way of thinking, it is striking chords in me left and right."

"What does it say?" asked Jean, marveling at how Bob had really perked up.

"Hard to explain really, but it is starting to ring some bells. I'm even beginning to see what might be happening to me," he said almost to himself. "Let me finish reading this chapter, and then, rather than trying to explain it, I'll let you read the first chapter. Then you'll see what I mean."

HIDDEN AGENDAS **At Work**

Once more Jean left him alone, but this time it was different. Something good was happening, she felt. But who had sent him that book? She went through a list in her own mind, but no one really popped out. Who might have cared enough to do it and then to remain anonymous?

Dennis

As soon as he got the news from Gwen Harper that Bob Pearson was having what Dennis interpreted as a nervous breakdown and wouldn't be back any time soon, he decided to make his move. He called an emergency meeting between the sales department and the production department to discuss what should be done in the light of the latest sales figures. He made it sound as though he and Bob had planned the meeting beforehand for this date, and that even though he couldn't be present, Bob nevertheless had given his blessing for the meeting to go ahead as planned.

Gwen Harper, of course, knew otherwise but kept silent and remained as invisible as possible. She would, however, take very careful minutes of the meeting. Dennis did not know that she knew so much about what was going on; he had always been somewhat oblivious with regard to her.

The **GiCo** Story

Monty Fisk vehemently protested about having the meeting at all, contending that the meeting was all one-sided since Mr. Pearson was really the person who directed the production side of the business, and he was not there to provide the strategic point of view.

Of course, Monty knew he was being set up by Dennis and that Dennis was out to get him this time. He knew his position was precarious without Bob Pearson there. His protests were in vain, however, and the meeting was fixed for later that same day.

Dennis had made a point of quietly appointing two or three loud-mouthed sales people he could rely on to spike the meeting with strong complaints. They would groan loudly about how production could never adequately service the contracts that the sales force created which meant complaints from customers and many lost sales.

He encouraged them to be as vociferous in their criticism of Monty Fisk as they liked and to point out, in no uncertain manner, how he refused to modernize and seemed unable to bring the company into the twenty-first century. That way, Dennis could stay above the fray, appearing to be only chairing the meeting, and, as usual, looking good.

Dennis began amicably, saying that the meeting was to be open and exploratory, without finger pointing on

HIDDEN AGENDAS At Work

either side. The aim was to see why the figures were down even though the economy was up and to have some discussion about ways of improving performance. But he knew he could depend on his sales staff to make trouble, since most of them had been against the production staff for many years. He knew they would be calling for blood.

It turned ugly very quickly, and the finger pointing started. And they all pointed at Monty Fisk. Monty knew then that, without Bob Pearson there, he was going to be "hung, drawn, and quartered" by everyone, including, it has to be said, some of his own staff; who seeing the way the wind was blowing, chose to support the winning side.

Monty was cornered and he knew it. He tried to rescue the situation by referring to plans that were in the works to improve production performance, a good many of which were already on Bob Pearson's desk awaiting his approval. He asked Dennis to adjourn the meeting pending the review of those plans.

Knowing that the damage was already done, Dennis graciously agreed and brought the meeting to a close, but not before an agreed statement of outcome was ratified that deplored the current situation and recognized the need for drastic action on the part of the production side to modernize and improve all systems as a matter of urgency. Nobody actually said as much, but the inference was that Monty was the problem and should be replaced.

It was a bad day for Monty Fisk. Gwen Harper couldn't help feeling sorry for him in spite of her own dislike. She could feel his loneliness and desperation and despised Dennis for setting Monty up the way he had. Meg, when she heard, felt much the same. Dennis, on the other hand, gloated. He'd had a good day.

Bob

Later that evening, Bob reluctantly relinquished the book to Jean, but only so she could read the first chapter, he was quick to point out. He was already two-thirds of the way through and wanted to finish it as soon as Jean had read at least some of it. However, by the time Jean had covered just a few pages, he had once again fallen into a deep, but now apparently restful sleep which was to last the whole night.

So Jean kept on reading and, like Bob, found the book to be both enlightening and at the same time disturbing. She was able to see how it related to both their lives. It started to give meaning to a number of things that had happened in their lives which, up until that moment, had seemed to both Bob and Jean, totally random and without any real meaning. According to this book, everything that happens has meaning and purpose and nothing is an accident.

To Jean, this was mind-blowing stuff. As she read on, she began to see how Bob had a pattern of creating failure over and over in his life, and that this latest episode was simply another repeat of the same thing. She also began to realize that the purpose of this breakdown was to heal something deep within himself that had caused him to keep failing virtually every five years.

Her eyes became heavy and soon she was lying beside her husband in as deep a sleep as he. But even as they slept, something was happening within them both.
Bob was awake early, at more or less his usual time. He went downstairs to make some coffee and took the book with him. By seven o'clock, he had completely finished it.

He went to his study, turned on the computer, and went straight to the web site given in the book. He logged into the online forgiveness worksheet, ready to try the process that was supposed to work almost instantaneously.

But whom to forgive? He remembered the e-mail that had come only a couple of days ago. Well, he thought,

The **GiCo** Story

why NOT Rick Tanner? Bob still had pain around that event even though it was many years ago. He would like to be free of it, for sure.

This form of forgiveness — Radical Forgiveness — was so different from traditional forgiveness that it really bore no relation to anything he had hitherto understood as forgiveness. So perhaps it might work with Rick Tanner. "Unlike traditional forgiveness, it is supposed to work almost instantaneously, so I'll soon find out," he reasoned to himself.

Bob spent the next hour and a half doing the online worksheet around Rick and the betrayal that he felt had occurred. The worksheet required that he write the story of what happened, to be the "victim" fully and to feel the feelings associated with the situation. Bob certainly was able to feel the anger and hurt, and he could feel the pain in his chest just like he had when that e-mail had arrived from Rick. But as he progressed through the worksheet, the pain in his chest subsided and the anger seemed to dissipate.

By the end of it, Bob felt more peaceful than he had in years. The pain was gone. Something had shifted in him and yet he didn't know what had shifted or why. It was a weird feeling. In response to a bunch of statements, he'd answered "willing," "open," "skeptical," or "unwilling" *(to accept),* but had not done much more

HIDDEN AGENDAS **At Work**

than that. "How could that have changed things so drastically?" he thought to himself. Just then Jean walked slowly down the stairs and came towards him.

"It's OK, Honey," he said quietly. "It's over. I'm on the mend. But, you know, I don't mean that in the sense of it's being business as usual. I have changed, and it feels good. I don't know what it means, but the whole world looks different to me now."

"I think I know what you mean," she whispered as she held him to her in a tender embrace. "I read a lot of the book myself last night as you slept. It's going to change both our lives."

"It's already changed mine," said Bob. "This morning, I went online and did a forgiveness worksheet on Rick Tanner. I'm not saying I like him any more than I did before, but the pain has gone. The betrayal — well, strangely enough, it doesn't seem like a betrayal any more. It seems like there was a higher purpose in it somehow; it's hard to explain."

"You don't have to," she replied. "I think I understand. After breakfast, I would like to do one for myself. There are a few people I need to forgive, too."

Later that morning, Bob put in a call to Gwen Harper. "Hello, Gwen, I'll be in around two o'clock this afternoon. Would you cancel that meeting I'm supposed to

The **GiCo** Story

be going to in New York on Friday of next week and book a flight to Atlanta instead for both Jean and me? We'll need to get there well before midday. We'll be there the whole weekend, so book us a flight back early on Monday morning. Thanks. See you at two."

Gwen Harper was dumbfounded. He sounded more up and alive than she'd heard him sound in years. Something had happened in the last couple of days, but she couldn't imagine what it was.

She put in a call to Monty Fisk but decided to forget to tell Dennis. She set to work preparing the minutes of the previous day's meeting so they would be ready on Bob's desk by the time he got in.

Bob came in right on time and went straight to his office. He read Mrs. Harper's report and immediately called her in. "Tell me what happened — and I want the whole story."

Bob listened carefully and fully understood what had occurred. He recognized it as an obvious ploy, not only to directly challenge his leadership, but to force Monty Fisk to come to Bob and call in the favor he always felt he was owed, thereby bringing it to everyone's attention.

This was no surprise to Bob since he had always known that Dennis would make a grab for the top job if the

HIDDEN AGENDAS At Work

opportunity ever cropped up. He understood that Dennis had absolutely no scruples about doing so — no matter who got hurt in the process.

Surprisingly, Bob felt neither angry, threatened nor upset. In fact he almost felt like laughing. He also found himself feeling sorry for Dennis that he should be so driven to carry out these kinds of schemes, hurting himself as well as others in the process. He made a few strategic calls and then called Dennis on the intercom.

"Hi, Dennis. I'm back. Would you come to my office please; right away?"

Dennis immediately went into shock, and for the first time in his life, was speechless. Gwen Harper had not told him that Bob was coming in today, and Dennis had convinced himself that it would be many days before Bob would return. To hear his voice strong and forceful on the phone was totally unnerving. He straightened his tie, took a deep breath and then made his way to Bob's office.

"Quite a stunt you pulled yesterday, Dennis," said Bob, leaning back in his chair, looking Dennis straight in the eye. "Well, it has cost you your job, and it might even have cost you your career."

The **GiCo** Story

Dennis said nothing, but went very pale. He just stared back at Bob in disbelief. This was not the Bob Pearson he knew.

"I have nothing against you personally, Dennis," Bob went on. "I only wish we could have worked together as a team, but for as long as I have known you, you have sought to create divisions within the firm purely to satisfy your own ambitions. You have soured relations between sales and production purely with the intent of undermining my position so you could jump into my shoes."

Dennis was about to protest his innocence, but Bob put up his hand and stopped him. "Did you really think I didn't know?" said Bob. "I have known all along that you would do anything to get this job away from me. You are totally transparent, Dennis.

"Because of the rifts you have caused, you have been very toxic and costly to this company, and I have grave doubts that you could ever change. I need to have people around me I can trust, Dennis, and you have given me plenty of reasons to think I can never trust you. I am therefore relieving you of your post effective immediately. We will work out a generous severance package for you in recognition of your years of service, but I need you out of here right now."

"You're firing me, Bob?" asked Dennis incredulously, leaning forward and slowly rising from his chair, unwinding like a snake about to strike.

But again, Bob was ready for him. He looked Dennis right in the eyes and shot back at him, "Yes, Dennis, you're fired. I'm sorry it has to be this way, but you brought it upon yourself. But listen to me, Dennis, and hear me good. As I said just now, this could be the end of your career — but it needn't be."

Bob paused, but kept looking straight at Dennis. "So long as you leave now, quietly, without making any fuss whatsoever," he continued, "I will help you get another position by giving you a decent reference. On the other hand, if you make things difficult around here — even for a day — I will see to it that you never work in this industry again. Do I make myself clear?"

Before Dennis could say anything, Bob went on, "Oh, and by the way, Dennis, I made my relationship with Monty Fisk known to the chairman right from the very start, even the bit about Monty's having tipped me off about the opening, so Monty never did have any leverage over me on that score at all. He may have thought so, just as you did, Dennis, but he really didn't. Ironic, isn't it?"

Dennis did not respond. By this time he had gone from deathly pale to deep red and purple, and he looked

The **GiCo** Story

as if he were about to explode. All the veins in his neck were standing out, and his eyes blazed with rage. But he knew that Bob had him hooked and literally held his future in his hands, so he knew better than to say all that was right there in his throat.

"I would like you to have your office cleared and be gone by the end of the day tomorrow. That's all, Dennis. Thank you."

Bob had felt calm during the exchange and remained so even after Dennis had walked out of the office without saying a word. Bob felt he had done the right thing both for the company and for Dennis. Bob felt good, not so much at having gotten rid of Dennis but at having found his own power again. The weekend workshop he had booked himself into in Atlanta was going to be good for him, and he knew it.

It was now time to talk to Monty Fisk before the news of Dennis' removal got around. Bob wanted to be the one to break that news to Monty.

When he did so, Bob let Monty have his moment of triumph and to express his relief. Then he went on to make it very clear to Monty that everyone who needed to know about the past knew everything there was to know, and that Monty should not count on any favors from Bob, either now or in the future.

HIDDEN AGENDAS **At Work**

He also put Monty on notice that the plans for modernization had better be good, or he might well be the next to go. Bob also made it clear that Monty must commit to working with the new person who would be appointed as sales and marketing vice-president. He had to create synergy and cooperation or, again, face the prospect of looking for another job.

Monty left Bob's office in a total daze. He had been delighted to hear about Dennis, but was completely shaken by everything else Bob Pearson had to say. He had never heard him be so direct and truthful, and Monty was left with no doubt as to his own vulnerability. Bob had made it very clear to him that he had to shape up or face the same fate as Dennis.

The Workshop Experience

Bob and Jean returned from Atlanta on Monday afternoon feeling great. Both of them felt revitalized and transformed by the experience. The workshop had given them and all the other participants the opportunity to go fully into their stories and to feel and express their feelings about what had happened in the past, or was happening to them now, before moving into a process of transformation around the whole thing.

The **GiCo** Story

Since both Rick Tanner and Dennis had brought forth betrayal issues for him, Bob told the group everything that had happened between him and those two people.

But the real work began, and his transformation came about, when he began sharing first about his dad and then his grandfather. He was given total permission to feel and express his anger around his dad which he did in a way that was both cathartic and freeing. Beneath that anger he discovered a terrible sadness that emanated from way deep down in his unconscious mind. The sadness came from knowing that the approval he so desperately needed from his father would always be denied him — because his father was incapable of giving it.

Bob finally recognized that reality and came to terms with it in a way that was totally liberating for him. He came to realize that he no longer needed anyone's approval and finally gave up his boyhood need for his father's. That was incredibly empowering for him.

He also reconnected with the grief he had repressed at age five, but was still there, about the loss of his grandfather and the guilt that was associated with not having been there when he died. Bob began to see how all of that was driving his life and how he himself was actually creating events in his life that replayed these events in symbolic form and confirmed his beliefs about himself, especially those put there by his emotionally wounded father.

HIDDEN AGENDAS **At Work**

He came to see how he symbolically recreated, over and over again, his grandfather's death, which had occurred when Bob was five years old. Every five years he would create a death of some kind, actual or symbolic, that would result in shame and grief.

The pattern was that everything would go well for a while and then fall apart around the five-year mark. He saw how Rick Tanner had actually helped him sabotage that big opportunity so that he could remain "right" about the idea that "my world always falls apart after five years" and the one about his "never amounting to anything." Rick abandoned Bob just as surely as Bob's grandfather had done by dying, and he made Bob feel totally inadequate just as Bob's father had done.

Bob saw how he had been setting himself up again to fail with GiCo, Inc. He was in his fifth year as president and, right on cue, everything was going downhill.

He learned that, through something he came to understand as Spiritual Intelligence, he had even, at some deep level — and just as he had done with Rick — 'recruited' Dennis to play the betrayal card again for him. Furthermore, that it was all purposeful in leading towards Bob's healing. In other words, Dennis didn't really do anything TO him; rather, he did it FOR him.

Upon learning this, he felt bad about firing Dennis. When he mentioned this in the workshop, he was told

The **GiCo** Story

that the gift always flows in both directions: that it was just as much a learning experience for Dennis as it was for Bob and that everything happens the way it should. Spiritual Intelligence, it seems, always keeps things in balance. Upon learning this, he was able to let that go and to know that, in any case, he had done the right thing for the company.

What the workshop did for Bob in the short term was to totally reprogram his belief system around his core-negative belief that he would "never amount to anything" and to neutralize the idea that "everything falls apart after five years." Not only did this save Bob Pearson, but it saved the company and all those in it. There was no reason for the company to slide downhill any more.

With regard to his father, it was to take Bob a number of years before coming to a place where he could truly forgive him, but even quite soon after the workshop, he noticed a significant difference in how his father acted towards him. Slowly and almost imperceptibly over the next few years, their relationship was to become more accepting — even a bit more loving.

Strangely enough, immediately after the workshop, Bob found himself feeling the need to reconnect with Rick Tanner. All the old anger and resentment had gone, and he really had warm feelings about Rick.

Bob kept thinking how strange it was that Rick had e-mailed him on his birthday after all that time. It was almost as if this whole roller-coaster of change and incredible growth had started with that e-mail. He really felt that Rick might have been one of the most important people in his life, but didn't quite understand why. Gwen Harper, though, could probably have told him.

Rick

The phone rang in Gwen Harper's office. Somehow she wasn't surprised to hear Rick Tanner's voice. "Hi Gwen. This is Rick. How are things over there these days?"
"Well, I don't know what you did, Rick Tanner, but it sure did have an effect. What did you do, you scoundrel?"

"Why?"

"Well, Mr. Pearson has suddenly come alive. He's a totally different person now. He's come into his power in a way I never thought possible. He sacked Dennis Barker on the spot after finding out that Dennis had tried to undermine him while he was away. He called Monty Fisk's bluff at long last and has taken charge of

The **GiCo** Story

the firm in a way that we have never seen before. Everyone's talking about it, and frankly, everyone is really excited. They feel like they have a leader again.

"So, Rick, what the hell did you do?"

"I sent Bob a book."

"What book?"

"Oh, just a self-help book."

"Well, it must have been one hell of a book to create that kind of change in someone like Bob Pearson. He's not normally the kind of guy to be into self-help. He's usually so rational and practical-minded."

"It sure sounded like he needed *any* kind of help when you called me that day, Gwen. I can tell you this — he was in the dark night of his soul right then. Believe me, I know. I've been there. And when you're in that place, there's only one kind of help that's possible, Gwen, and that's spiritual help."

"Wow, you've changed, Rick Tanner. I never thought I'd hear you talking about spiritual matters. I know I haven't seen you in a while, but you seem different. What happened to you, Rick?. Was it when you and Barbara broke up?"

HIDDEN AGENDAS **At Work**

"Can't go into it now, Gwen. Suffice it to say, I was forced to grow up and to face myself. What I saw, I didn't like, so I set about discovering what it was about me that made me act like a jerk. I went to the same workshop that Bob went to last week, and it changed my life.

"How did you know that Mr. Pearson went to a workshop last week?" Gwen demanded to know.

"I have my sources," Rick replied.

"Well, don't quote me as one of your sources, Rick Tanner. I still don't trust you, you old fart. But, seriously, I am grateful for what you did for Mr. Pearson. It sure did seem to be exactly what was needed. I am impressed, Rick, really I am."

"I'm glad it did the trick, Gwen, but really, it wasn't me. I only followed my intuition. I was told what to do, and I did it. That's it."

Gwen put the phone down and had to wonder to herself how so much could change so radically in such a short time. In spite of it all she felt exhilarated.

Bob

While at the workshop in Atlanta, Bob had been excited to learn that there was a way to bring a version of the new technology he had experienced to the entire company. It was called *The Quantum Energy Management System* (QEMS). He felt that it would help to mend the rift that Dennis Barker had created between the departments, restore relationships, and reinvigorate the whole company.

He had come to understand how each and every person in the company brought their core-negative beliefs, their wounds, and their unconscious grief to work with them. That's exactly what he had done.

In order to deal with that, the QEMS system installs some simple processes and tools into the corporate structure that prevent such energies taking hold. It helps an individual or group automatically dissolve whatever is coming up to be acted out.

He knew enough about Monty's background to understand now why he was giving Meg Smith such a hard time. She obviously reminded him, at some deep unconscious level, of his mother. Bob determined that he would offer to send Monty to the workshop he had just attended in the hope that Monty's dynamic with his mother would be healed. Then he wouldn't keep

HIDDEN AGENDAS **At Work**

acting it out over and over again with people like Meg. He also decided in that moment to offer Meg the opportunity to become the QEMS Coordinator. Promotion for her was well overdue, he thought, mainly due to Monty Fisk's interference. She was caring and empathetic but at the same time could be firm and effective. She was bright and everyone respected her, so she was perfect for the job.

Bob immediately put a call in to Helen Barnes, the director of human resources, to confer with her about it. Helen concurred and agreed to let Monty Fisk know of their decision. Fortunately, Helen had someone in mind who could take Meg's place, so continuity would not be a problem for the production department.

Meg

Meg left Bob's office in an absolute whirl. She'd had no idea why Mr. Pearson had sent for her. Monty had been stone-faced about it when he had relayed the message he'd received from Gwen Harper that Bob wanted to see her. She'd intuited that Monty knew what was about to happen, but he wasn't letting on, so Meg had no idea whether it was good or bad. However, when she had arrived at Gwen Harper's desk, Gwen winked at her and let Meg know by her expression that all was well as she ushered Meg into Bob's office.

The **GiCo** Story

Meg stood outside Bob's office looking at the pack of information he had just given her. She was to become the coordinator of this new employee development system? Although Bob had tried to explain it all to her, she really had not taken it in and did not have a grasp of what she was being promoted into. However, she had certainly grasped the fact that at last she would be free of Monty Fisk. She also felt very good about the fact that she would be earning quite a bit more money.

"Congratulations, my dear," purred Gwen knowingly. Since her conversation with Rick, she now knew that the events of the last few days, including Meg's promotion, were the result of her fateful decision to put that call in to Rick Tanner. Exactly how it had all transpired, other than the fact that Rick had sent Bob that book, she didn't really know, but she was ready to take credit for being the one to start the whole thing. "You deserve it, Meg."

"Did you have something to do with this, Mrs. Harper?" asked Meg, recalling their lunchtime conversation only a few days back.

"Not really," replied Gwen. "If I did anything at all, it was only tangentially. No, Mr. Pearson made the decision entirely on his own and then conferred with Helen Barnes, who agreed immediately."

"What about Mr. Fisk?" Meg wondered out loud. "I wonder how he'll take it?"

"Don't worry about Monty Fisk," replied Gwen, somewhat gleefully. "Mr. Pearson had him in there a while ago, and I think he took the wind right out of Monty's sails. Monty came out of that office with his tail between his legs. I don't think he'll be giving you any more grief from now on."

Meg walked into Monty's office. "Congratulations, Meg," he told her. "I hear you're moving into the human resources department, and that it's a promotion, right?"

"That's right. They have actually created a new post for me, but as yet, I don't fully understand what it entails," replied Meg, unable to read where Monty was coming from or how he felt about the situation. It was as if they were dancing around each other, like a couple of Aikido fighters, each one waiting for the other to make a move. There was a long pause.

"I'm pleased for you, Meg," Monty finally said, without meeting her eyes. "I'll miss you."

"Thanks," said Meg quietly, not knowing what else to say, and she left the room. She was quite sure, however, that her dance with Monty Fisk was not yet over, not by a long shot.

Bob

Bob decided that he would call a meeting of the whole company the next day. He would use it to formally announce Dennis Barker's departure, introduce the idea of bringing in the new energy management system, announce Meg's appointment as the program coordinator, and explain why he felt this was necessary for the ongoing health of GiCo, Inc.

He wanted to use the meeting to launch his new vision for the company and to firmly establish his leadership once and for all. When Bob walked into the meeting, he felt strong, determined and excited, better than he had felt for years.

> "Good morning everyone. I don't intend to keep you long, but I have called this meeting to personally bring you up to date on what has happened in the last week or so, to share some plans with you, and to give you some assurances about our future. As you may already have heard, Dennis Barker has left the company after a successful tenure as vice president of sales and marketing, and we have retained an executive search company to find a replacement for him. In the meantime, Jim Baker has agreed to step in as acting vice-president, and I know you will give him your total support. Thank you, Jim. We are certainly sorry to see Dennis go

and wish to express our gratitude for his long and valuable service to this company, and we genuinely wish him well as he moves on to new horizons.

"At this time I would like to update you on the new course that I am setting for the company — not only towards greater growth and development but with a clear vision of how we should achieve that in the best possible way for all concerned. We have some exciting new plans for modernizing the production department which we will be laying before you within a couple of months and asking for your input.

"I can share with you that I recently went through a very difficult time — personally — as we all do. However, I was fortunate enough to find a program that helped me see what was going on in my life that needed to change, not only at home, but at work too.

"As I thought about my work and how this company should be run, I realized that for a company to be strong, to be powerful, to be prosperous and to make a contribution, it needs to be founded on genuine teamwork. That doesn't just mean being efficient; it means supporting each other as human beings and helping each other be the best we can be — as people. People are at their best and contributing the most when they are happy and aligned with

The **GiCo** Story

each other, and I intend for that to be a priority from now on.

"This company has suffered from interdepartmental rivalry of a very negative nature. This has caused a lot of unhappiness. I have seen enough of the subterfuge and the use of divide-and-rule tactics, and I will not tolerate that kind of behavior any more. It caused us to leak energy — human energy — and that is wasteful. Human energy is a basic resource that has to be used wisely, so when we leak human energy, we lose in every other way too. We lose morale; we lose productivity; we lose profitability; we lose markets.

"The company leaks human energy when people are not happy in their work or feel frustrated. We lose energy when we fail to promote cooperation and respect for our individual fellow worker. The single most important way that this company has been leaking energy over the last few years is through the interdepartmental conflict I have just mentioned. You all know what I am talking about.

"This kind of negative rivalry has been allowed to fester in this company for too long. In fact, I would go so far as to say that it has actually been encouraged by some managers with agendas of their own. When departments feel adversarial towards each other and seek to undermine each other, everyone loses.

"I will not tolerate this kind of thing any longer, and I need everyone to be on notice that if I see or hear of anyone engaging in this kind of behavior in the future, they will be placed on written final warning immediately. That said, of course, I am aware that no one can mandate a change of attitudes through edict, and I know that change cannot be brought about by threats or fear tactics.

"I am therefore instituting some new policies and training programs to help us become an organization where people treat each other with mutual respect, openness and caring and where people feel valued for who they are and don't feel the need to put others down so they can feel OK.

"I want this to be a healthier place to work because the truth is that when everyone feels good about being here, and in tune with their fellow workers, they will give of their best and we will all win.

"To that end, I am bringing in a training company that will help us make these kinds of changes over a period of six to twelve months. Everyone in the company will be involved, including myself, of course, and all the management personnel, staff and production people. If we are going to make these changes and reap the rewards, we must all be committed to the effort.

"The program they will implement will help us manage our own energy and have it be in alignment with company goals. It will help us plug the leaks and maximize everyone's contribution to the flow of productive energy throughout the firm."

Moving to a flip chart, Bob continued.

"If I can just explain this a little further — there are four main types of energy running through any company. The first is information or data. The second is materials and products. The third is money and the fourth is human energy.

"When human energy is not properly channeled or is misdirected, as in our case through interdepartmental fighting, it can block the flow of these other three here, and everyone loses. If it is properly directed, it can enhance the energy flow of the other three and everyone wins.

"This new program will help us to learn how to refine the flow of human energy not just to improve the bottom line, which it will, of course, but at the same time to make this a happier workplace for everyone.

"At the personal level, I will not be asking any of you to do anything I am not demanding of myself. I have recently taken a personal training, given by these same people, that has changed how I see my own life and how I relate to other people at home and at work.

"But the difference between this training and every other program I have experienced was that it gave me tools — tools that help me to get through the difficult moments and challenges that life throws at me that ordinarily would keep me stuck.

"Fortunately for us, the technology is equally applicable and helpful to groups of people, especially groups of people who work together. So, you will get those same tools to help you deal with problems in your own life that you would otherwise bring to work, as well as to improve your relationships at work.

"As I said, everyone will be involved, no matter where they work, because the idea is to give everyone in the company a way of working together and resolving issues that everyone understands thoroughly and can apply easily in any situation.

"In its simplest form, you might think of it as a sophisticated system of conflict resolution and prevention. It certainly is that and we shall be

The **GiCo** Story

using it for that purpose and benefiting from it in that regard, but it is much more.

"It is, in fact, a way to create a very special form of synergy and workplace harmony such that it magnifies the productive energy of each and every individual in the company. Everyone benefits — emotionally as well as financially. I think you are going to really appreciate the results.

"I am confident that, by embracing this system, we will all come together in a wholly new way. I think it will help us, not only to recapture the same kind of family atmosphere that once prevailed at this company, where everyone cared about everyone else, but to take that idea of caring to a whole new level. I want every person in this company to feel that they belong here and that this is a place where they feel supported physically, emotionally and spiritually.

"Let me be clear about this. I am not trying to recreate the past. Neither am I indulging in sentimental nostalgia about days that were part of a bygone age. Nor am I saying that in order to have a family atmosphere we need to stay the size we are now. Absolutely not. What I am talking about here is a modern, cutting-edge technique that enables us to manage our own individual energy so that we can each give of our best for the company and, at the same time, feel personally fulfilled.

"This technology can be applied to any company whatever its size and indeed, far from keeping us the size we are, I believe it will help us to become more productive and more successful and, consequently, enable us to grow and expand in a way that has not been possible in the past.

"I want the negativity of the past to fade away as soon as possible and for us now to embrace a policy of inclusion, cooperation, sharing and mutual support. This won't happen overnight — I am well aware of that. We all have learning to do and changes to make in our attitudes, ways of thinking and ways of being. But this new technology, as long as we all embrace and agree to use it, will move us in this direction.

"As an indication of our commitment to this program, Helen Barnes and I have decided to create a new management position for someone to coordinate the whole program. I am delighted to announce that we have asked Meg Smith to be that coordinator, and she has accepted the position. Monty Fisk will miss her, I am sure, but we feel that she is perfect for the job of implementing this program and training everyone to use it to the best possible advantage.

"Meg will be taking quite a bit of training in the technology, in the next week or two herself, to get thoroughly acquainted with the program and the use of the tools, and she will then be disseminating information to everyone. She will be arranging the seminars that will mark the beginning of the program and, once the program is running, will be the person we all refer to for help with using the tools as and when required. Those seminars will take place in about two months, off the premises but nearby and on the firm's time."

Bob dealt with a few more items of business and then brought the meeting to a close. After he left, the room was buzzing, everyone wondering what it was all to mean for them. They hadn't totally understood what Bob was talking about, but it didn't matter. Whatever it was, it sounded good.

One man from sales and marketing summed it up. "We've got Bob Pearson back, that's for sure. I don't know where we're going, but at least we're on the road again!"

Rick

The phone rang at 7:45 a.m. That was not a time at which Rick was usually wide awake and lucid. "Hello," he mumbled into the mouthpiece, wondering who might be calling at this hour.

HIDDEN AGENDAS **At Work**

"Hi, Rick, this is Bob — Bob Pearson. Happy belated fiftieth birthday greetings. How are you?"

"Hey, Bob!" shouted Rick. "What's going on, old buddy?"

Bob was silent for a moment or two at the other end, and Rick wondered what might be coming next. "It was you, wasn't it?" said Bob Pearson quietly. "You sent me that book, Rick, didn't you?"

"I thought it might help, Bob. I didn't want to interfere, but I heard that you were in bad shape, so I did the only thing I knew to do. Did it help at all?"

"Rick, I'd like to take you up on your e-mail invitation to get together for lunch or something. What are you doing today?"

"I'm free. What time and where?" asked Rick.

They agreed on time and place and ended the conversation. Rick replaced the receiver and sank back under the covers, wondering what the day might bring. It had been a long time since he and Bob had been together, and Rick couldn't help noticing that he was feeling apprehensive about the meeting.

When Bob hadn't answered his e-mail, Rick had virtually written off all possibility of their ever healing the relationship. But when Gwen Harper had called out of the blue and told him that Bob was close to having what she thought was a nervous breakdown, he somehow understood what Bob needed. That was because, some two years prior, Rick Tanner had gone through his dark night of the soul and knew the signs. He also knew Bob Pearson well enough to know that Bob would have buried his pain and that it would take a breakdown of sorts to bring him to his senses.

Rick's dark night of the soul had come as a consequence of his creating cancer. When he was diagnosed, he had two golf-ball-sized tumors in his right lung and a smaller one in his left.

The doctors hadn't given him much of a chance, but they wanted to give him chemotherapy anyway. Rick didn't know what to do. He asked the doctors for some time to think it over. They didn't like it, but Rick always got his way.

Not long after his initial diagnosis, Rick was attending a conference. He had booked late and so was having to share a room with someone who just happened to be a doctor. He had been pretty mad about having to do that, since Rick liked his own space and was used to having everything he wanted, but he'd had no choice in the matter this time. As it happened, the doctor was hardly ever in the room, so they didn't have to interact much.

HIDDEN AGENDAS **At Work**

During the conference Rick was in a lot of pain and having difficulty breathing. On the second night, he awoke at about 3:00 a.m. struggling to get a breath.

His heart was racing, and he was sweating profusely. The noise and commotion he was making woke his roommate who, upon seeing Rick's condition, jumped out of bed and came over to Rick. "What's up, my friend?" he said. "Can I help you?"

All Rick could do was to point to his chest and get the words "lung cancer" out in between gasps for breath.

The conference was taking place in a retreat center a long way from any hospital, and the doctor had no drugs or other tools of his profession with him since it wasn't a medical conference. In any case, he was no longer practicing regular medicine.

He put his hands over Rick's chest and held them there. Within a few moments Rick's heart slowed down and his breathing got progressively easier. After ten minutes or so, Rick settled into a deep sleep. The doctor washed his hands under cold running water and got back into bed.

When Rick awoke the next morning, the doctor was gone. All his personal things were gone too, so obviously he wasn't coming back.

"Who was that man?" Rick thought. "And what did he do to me last night? I'm feeling so much better!" He was breathing easier and he had no pain.

He even wondered whether he had dreamed the whole thing. Then he noticed an envelope on his bedside table. When he opened it and read the note, he knew he hadn't dreamt it.

Friend,

I believe your tumors may have gone, at least for now. But they will come back soon if you don't soften your heart and tear down the walls you have built up around your heart. Forgive everyone and everything, especially yourself. Love heals everything.

The Doc

Two Years Later

Looking back over the two years since Bob had his dark night of the soul *(he still talked about it as simply a bout of nervous exhaustion but, really, he knew better)*, he could hardly believe the changes that had taken place at GiCo. Of course, Rick's having invested twenty-five million dollars into

HIDDEN AGENDAS **At Work**

the company to facilitate the modernization had made things a lot easier, but even so, it had been an interesting two years.

The new program had been introduced, and Meg Smith had certainly turned out to be a great coordinator for it. She had organized the two-day training seminars that everyone had attended in groups over a period of time and had developed a sixth sense about when people might be needing to use the tools that came with it. She kept everyone motivated to use the tools for their own personal issues and for when issues looked like they might be arising in the work situation.

Bob had made it a condition that every applicant for Dennis Barker's position had to be in total agreement with the new workplace policy. He meant with regard to the way working relationships were handled and fostered through the use of the new program. They also had to be committed to their own growth.

Well, Bob had found just that kind of person in John Peterson, who had turned out to be an excellent VP of sales and marketing. John had united his team very quickly and had increased sales by 24 percent in the first year and around 15 percent in the second.

Finding common cause with Monty Fisk, he and Monty together had instituted some radical changes in how the departments worked with each other. This had led

The **GiCo** Story

to some great innovations in production technology which, of course, Rick's twenty-five million had helped to implement. Nevertheless, Bob knew that the money was secondary. It was the alignment of the human energy within and between the departments that drove the changes and made them effective.

Three of the five people in the sales department who had aligned themselves with Dennis Barker's divide-and-rule policy had left within a very short time of the new policies being introduced. Interestingly, they were the ones who had been creating the most trouble at that fateful meeting two years ago.

The other two came to be among the staunchest supporters of the new approach and had been promoted several times. One of them, Colin Smith, was now John Peterson's director in place of Jim Baker, who also had left soon after the changes. Jim simply couldn't handle the new way of operating. Colin Smith had been one of those who had made it uncomfortable for Monty at that meeting, but over the last eighteen months or so, they had become good friends.

Bob had sent Monty to the same workshop he had attended and it had worked wonders for Monty. It had helped him completely resolve his issues around his overprotective mother and to release all the core-negative beliefs about himself and life that had kept him stuck all those years.

HIDDEN AGENDAS At Work

Meg Smith also did the workshop as a prerequisite to becoming the QEMS Coordinator. In the end, she and Monty actually developed quite a close relationship.

At the first sign of any disturbance in the emotional equilibrium of his department, he would send people to Meg so she could help them with using the special tools and take a keen interest in how they fared. The supervisor that took Meg's place was an older woman, but she and Monty got on very well.

Eighteen months after the program had been implemented, Monty was offered a job as production manager of a much larger company at a considerably higher salary and had accepted it. Bob had given him a glowing testimonial, especially since he knew that the job was more suited to Monty's background and training.

Monty had done well in computerizing his production system at GiCo but this new firm was still fairly traditional in its approach and it would suit Monty much better. Much to Bob's surprise, Monty was there only six months before he met and subsequently married one of his staff.

GiCo had become stronger by far and had grown into a company employing more than two hundred people. Bob marveled at how all the people that had been resistant to the new approach from the beginning had

The **GiCo** Story

left and been replaced by people who loved the idea and fitted right into it. Bob was quite sure that everyone in the company was now aligned with it.

Who wouldn't enjoy working for a company that was committed to the happiness and the overall mental, emotional and spiritual health of its workers? The word had gotten around, and other company leaders were asking Bob what he had done to make things so different at GiCo in just two years.

Gwen Harper was still his personal assistant and was as loyal as ever to him. She never would go and do a workshop, even when Bob offered to pay for her, but she got a lot out of the company seminars that Meg organized and sometimes ran. She had become much less reclusive and a whole lot less picky and judgmental in the last two years. People really liked her and always looked to her for advice. She remained the matriarch of the secretarial staff, of course, and continued to keep her ear to the ground for anything interesting.

Bob had heard on the grapevine that Dennis Barker had apparently done reasonably well for himself and was head of sales with another small company in a town pretty far away. Fortunately, Bob had never been asked for a reference. One would have been due since Dennis had not made any kind of a fuss leaving GiCo, as he might well have done had Bob not threatened him on that point. Bob was thankful for not having to pen a recommendation, for it would have been a difficult and delicate task.

Rick Tanner rarely came by and even then only to meet with Bob for a drink or a meal out together. He had invested his money with no strings attached and made absolutely no demands on Bob. He wanted no part in the running of the business except as a board member, and in fact, seldom ever spoke about the business. His passion lay in his work as a spiritual counselor and Radical Forgiveness coach, and, of course, he and Bob could now relate to one another on this level in a way that would have been impossible before.

Rick and Bob had spent more than three hours that first day over lunch talking about the true meaning of what had occurred for each of them over the years, in light of the philosophy given in the book Rick had sent and from what Bob had learned from the workshop he had attended. Rick had, of course, attended two of those same workshops some two years prior to Bob's doing so.

It had not been until a month or so later, and after their friendship had been totally renewed and a strong bond based on trust and mutual respect had been established, that Rick asked Bob if he could invest in GiCo, Inc., to help with the modernization. There would be no favors expected, and he'd prefer that most people

The **GiCo** Story

not know about it. He especially didn't want Meg Smith to know that he had anything to do with the company. He felt sure that she hated him.

Mainly through Gwen Harper, Rick had discreetly kept up with how Meg Smith was doing, and he was especially interested in Caroline. One day she and Rick ran into each other in the grocery store. To his surprise she seemed pleased to see him and was in no hurry to break away. Rick suggested they go for coffee, and she accepted.

They spent some hours together catching up and talking about her new role as QEMS coordinator and his new vocation as a spiritual counselor. Naturally they found that they had a lot in common since both their careers were grounded in the same way of seeing things.

Bob was best man at their wedding six months later. Caroline was the bridesmaid. Jean Pearson organized the reception and virtually everyone from the company was there to celebrate. So was Monty Fisk.

THE END

Humenergy Dynamics at GiCo — An Analysis

In writing the GiCo story, my aim was to show how latent, negatively charged *humenergy* might surface at work and become acted out between people who worked together. However, the story did take on a life of its own, so I thought it might be fun to briefly look back and analyze how *humenergy* seemed to be operating in the GiCo story and to what effect. But first, a couple of general points.

Typical or Not
I would not be surprised if you thought that the lives of the characters in the story were not typical, in that they all seem to have had abusive and/or alcoholic parents and less than perfect childhoods. Well, of course, I needed to have characters like that in order to make the story juicy, but the sad truth is that a lot of children grow up in abusive households. Abuse associated with alcoholism, as well as that which is not, iis much more common than most people realize. That's because it is swept under the carpet and vehemently denied by family members.

HIDDEN AGENDAS At Work

Meg's experience of trying to tell her mother about being sexually abused by her father, and getting shamed even more for daring to suggest such a thing, is quite typical. Research indicates that at least one in five adults in America today experienced physical or sexual abuse as a child, not to mention abuse of a verbal and emotional nature.

Having said that though, it is not only abused or wounded people who bring their *humenergy* to work with them. We all do. There isn't a human being on the planet who is without some toxic *humenergy*, and there will be times when we will wear it to work.

Complexity

Even though we limited our story to just four or five players and only touched on a tiny part of what might have been present for all of them, the dynamics were nevertheless complex, subtle and difficult to fathom.

Imagine trying to plot the dynamics where you have twenty or thirty players in close professional interaction on a daily basis, all acting out their core-negative beliefs and endeavoring to heal their primal wounds in the context of the workplace. It would be an impossibly complex web. Without some technology that uses Spiritual Intelligence — a form of intelligence we are not accustomed to using — it would be impossible to do anything about it.

Humenergy Dynamics

Overall Energy Field of GiCo, Inc.
To get back to the details of the story, there were obviously some problems with the corporate energy field dating back to the departure of the previous president. There were also some deep-rooted energy blocks existing between the sales and production departments that were not being addressed. On the contrary, these blocks were being actively and overtly fed by at least one of the executives, Dennis Barker, in his effort to overthrow Bob Pearson.

That dynamic alone put a huge dent in the corporate energy field, representing an energy leak of major proportion. Morale in the company was low, and the staff were registering an awareness of Bob Pearson's downwardly spiraling performance as their president.

Overall, the vibration of the company energy field was down and not conducive to high performance. Conflict, uncooperative behavior, high turnover, absenteeism, insubordination, apathy, cynicism and dissent were probably the order of the day. Energy was leaking everywhere from the company.

Individual Energy Fields
Let's now turn our attention to each of the individuals in the story and look at how each one's own *humenergy* fed into the dynamics of the company and, indeed, how the company itself served as fertile ground for their healing opportunities to arise.

HIDDEN AGENDAS **At Work**

Remember, what we are looking for is evidence, albeit very subtle and almost always inconclusive, that Spiritual Intelligence is working in our lives, always providing opportunities for us to heal and grow. Since we don't yet have the sight to directly observe this intelligence in operation, the best we can do is look for clues that might imply that it is. The kind of clues we look for are:

- a) Repeating patterns — similar events recurring
- b) Number patterns like dates, intervals, ages, etc.
- c) Oddities — things that just don't fit
- d) Synchronicities — used to be called coincidences
- e) Evidence of core-negative beliefs being lived out

Clues such as these give us reason to believe that there is an intelligence behind what seems to be occurring because the likelihood of such things happening by chance is extremely low.

Timelines Reveal the Patterns

One of the best ways to see the patterns is to plot timelines from birth to the present time, plotting any significant events that occurred along the way. Since we have the most biographical information on Bob Pearson and Meg Smith, let's do one for each of them.

In each case, the timelines offer interesting patterns that reveal the *humenergy* that each was bringing to work with them.

Bob's Timeline

50	--Dark night of the soul
45	--Bob joins GiCo
40	--Bob joins HEH.
30	--Rick's betrayal
25	--Bob and Rick's partnership
20	--Bob begins career
5	--Grandfather dies aged 51.

Bob's life was shaped by two main forms of primal wounding. The first was the mental and emotional abuse by his father. The second was the "abandonment" by his grandfather who died when Bob was five, compounded by Bob's own guilt and feelings of responsibility for the death.

Look at all the fives here!

Bob's core-negative beliefs were (a) he would never really measure up and be good enough, no matter how hard he tried and (b) his world would always fall apart after five years.

His pattern became creating three to four years of relative success with disaster setting in at year five. This kind of pattern is extremely common.

Rick also abandoned and betrayed Bob abruptly after five years and probably represented the brother to whom Bob was always adversely compared by his father.

It is interesting to note that Bob came face to face with his own death, even though it was symbolic, at more or less the same age at which his grandfather had died. An oddity? This is not unusual. Had Bob continued on the path he was taking, he might well have died physically right on cue the following year.

Meg's Timeline

Age	Event	
35	--Present	The primal wound that shaped Meg's life was the sexual abuse at age three. Notice how the number three (or multiples thereof) feature in her life story, mostly as intervals in years between related events.
34	--Divorces	
32	--CFS	Abused at 3, shamed by mother at 12, raped at 24, affair with Rick at 27. Married twice for three years and three year intervals between bouts of Chronic Fatigue Syndrome (CFS). This is a very typical pattern for an abuse victim.
31	--Marries #2	
29	--CFS	She was used and abused by her father, by a rapist, and by both husbands. Even though she decided to avoid men, she "created" Monty, who did the same.
28	--Divorces	
27	--Caroline born. Joins GiCo	Remember, he, inexplicably it seemed, turned on her after three years (an oddity). Even he couldn't understand why, but she, in effect, had recreated her father in Monty, and was acting out again the power struggle that had ensued when she reached age three. Monty, for his part, was acting out his rage with his mother.
26	--Meets Rick.	
25	--Marries	
24	--Raped	Her CFS was probably related to having been raised by an obsessive-compulsive and ultra-critical mother who made her believe that whatever she did would never be enough.
16	--Meg leaves home	That is a typical belief underlying CFS. People with CFS invariably had perfectionist mothers. Their belief: "No matter how hard I try, I'll never be enough."
12	--Meg confronts mother	
3	--Meg is abused by father	

Humenergy Dynamics

The Impact
Let's now look at the latent *humenergy* that was acted out at work by each of the players in this story and make an assessment of how it impacted the company they worked for.

Bob — A Danger to GiCo's Survival
Most of Bob's *humenergy* was revealed in the foregoing story, but basically he was acting out, every five years, the trauma of losing his grandfather when Bob was five and the belief that he had formed at that age, namely, that everything would fall apart after five years. The reason that his grandfather was so important to Bob is that he was his only source of love and approval.

The interesting thing here is that, but for Bob's natural intelligence and strong unconscious need to succeed in order to gain his father's approval, he would have been stuck in a downward spiral of failure. As it was, his native wit and foresight had somehow saved him on each occasion, usually by creating a sideways move just before the world crashed in on him. In that way, he had managed to keep operating at a fairly high level in the corporate world. He also, as far as we know, did not have failure with his women.

It was male energy that deserted him. There's nothing more masculine than a corporation. A corporation failed him every five years. What we don't know, of course, is what happened to HEH, Inc., when Bob bailed after having brought it to its low point. He may have ruined the company for all we know. On the other hand, having served Bob by enabling him to recreate his failure scenario, HEH, Inc. may have revived itself immediately.

Without a doubt, Bob Pearson was an extremely dangerous proposition for GiCo. On paper, and in person, he appeared to be an ideal candidate to lead any small or medium-sized company. No one would ever suspect that he had a powerful unconscious need to bring any company he worked for to its knees, simply in order that he could be right about his core-negative belief. He, himself, would never have suspected it either.

But that is where he and GiCo were headed, for sure, and disaster would probably have occurred had he not been exposed to the kind of technology that neutralized the core-negative belief. It is a chilling tale, but it happens all the time.

Dennis

Clearly the more seniority a person has in the company, the more effect their *humenergy* has. Dennis Barker's latent *humenergy*, based on and energized at the deepest level by his subconscious shame about his family and his roots, fueled his insatiable need to be number one. Clearly that need was toxic to the company. He created disharmony and sowed the seeds of discontent wherever and whenever he could in order to undermine Bob Pearson.

Meg

Seniority is not the only measure of how damaging *humenergy* can be. Meg was junior but her *humenergy* was potent, albeit more subtle than Bob's. Her core-negative belief, stemming from her abuse, required that she create men who would turn on her after about three years. She had given up on romantic associations since they all had done just that. So, having failed to see the gift in the romantic associations, she (her Spiritual Intelligence) had "enrolled" Monty Fisk to play that role for her so she might finally heal her original wound. (She eventually did when she found QEMS.)

Not only was the relationship between Monty and Meg counterproductive in itself, but it created a lot of dissent and trouble among the staff. Consequently, a great deal of energy was being lost through that department. It's hard to believe that this was purely the result of Meg's unconscious need to heal her abuse and Monty's willingness to play out the role of abuser, isn't it?

Monty

As for Monty Fisk himself, his *humenergy* was centered around his hatred of his overbearing mother, so it was not difficult for him to be abusive to Meg, since to him, at some deep unconscious level, she represented his mother. Aged forty-six, Monty had never married because of his hatred of women in general, but he did so within six months of doing QEMS. Meg did the same!

Gwen

Gwen Harper was a walking time bomb. So long as she was on your side, her *humenergy* worked for you and for the company. Her need to be the caretaker, as well as her ability to be invisible but vigilant, all worked to make her a good executive secretary. But anyone who as much as hinted that women were not as important as men or who tried to undermine those for whom she felt responsible needed to look out!

Synchronicities

Interesting synchronicities occur between Gwen, Rick, Meg and Bob. Gwen was able to connect the dots. Had it not been for those connections and Gwen's need to take care of Bob and Meg, as well as to intuit what needed to be done, the call to Rick would not have been made. Who knows what might have happened to Bob — and GiCo, Inc. — then? And, of course, there was that doctor who saved Rick's life. Who *was* that man?

Using QEMS Technology
For Our Own Soul Survival at Work

Originally the QEMS technology was designed to be used, if not by every person in the organization, then at least by the top tier of management. I always saw it as a 'top-down' system — one that was totally supported and used by the CEO and his/her management team.

However, we have since realized that it can also be used by any individual in the organization for their own personal benefit. *(See page 121 for details of the benefits.)* It was clear, too, that an individual using the tools would have a positive impact on the energy field of the organization.

QEMS was, after all, founded upon the technology of Radical Forgiveness, which is primarily an individualized system of dissolving negative energy (*humenergy*) from one's own energy field. It is done privately and within oneself and yet others around us are affected by our shift in energy, especially those with whom we have forgiveness issues.

HIDDEN AGENDAS At Work

So we are now marketing the QEMS kit to individuals, confident that its use will not only make a huge difference to the person using it, but will have an effect, albeit in a subtle way, on the organization itself.

The "Q-Work" Kit
The Q-Work Kit is simply a set of tools for balancing one's energy. Just as the success of Radical Forgiveness resulted almost entirely from the fact that we supplied a range of tools to do the forgiveness work, the same is true of the Quantum Energy Management System.

Without the tools to activate one's Spiritual Intelligence, QEMS would just be a nice idea, but it would change nothing. Shifting subtle energies in one's consciousness requires the use of tools that connect not with one's mental intelligence, nor even one's emotional intelligence, but with our Spiritual Intelligence.

Tools
The Q-Work kit contains a number of tools that one would use whenever there is a situation occurring that is clearly the result of some *humenergy* coming to the surface and getting acted out. It might be theirs or someone else's; it doesn't matter so long as they are involved to some extent in the drama. This is important because the only person's energy they can change is their own. It cannot be done on behalf of another. If someone is involved, even if only peripherally, they

use the tools to shift the energy within themselves. This nevertheless has the effect of shifting the energy in the entire situation.

No one needs to know the individual has done, or is doing the Q-Work around the situation. Even if they did, they wouldn't connect it with the situation having "mysteriously" resolved itself — unless they were in the program themselves, of course. That's why we are referring to the use of the Q-Work Kit by individuals as a *'stealth'* system and the people who choose to work it as *'stealth energy shifters.'*

The "Q-Work" Kit

The kit contains the following items:

- The Q-Work Journal
- Booklet — How to Use the QEMS Technology
- Pad of Balancing *Humenergy* Worksheets
- Book — *Spiritual Intelligence at Work.*
- Book — *Quantum Healing Thru RF**
- CD — Introduction to QEMS and Q-Work
- CD — The GiCo Story, read by the author
- CD — Jill's Story, with introduction and analysis
- CD — The Q-Work Tools
- CD — How to Use the Balancing *Humenergy* Worksheet

* This is a shortened version of the book that started it all — *Radical Forgiveness: Making Room for the Miracle.* This is the one that Rick sent Bob Pearson. Available at www.radicalforgiveness.com

The three most important elements of the kit are the Online Interactive *Humenergy* Balancer, the Balancing *Humenergy* Worksheet, and the Q-Work Tools CD. This CD contains two instruments:

(a) The "Satori" Balancing Process. This takes about fifteen minutes and is done while sitting in a chair with eyes closed.

(b) The 13 Steps to Radical Forgiveness Process. This takes about seven minutes, and can be done with eyes open.

The 13 Steps process is one that can be done while driving since all it requires is a "yes" response to 13 questions, and there is no need to have one's eyes closed to do it. A lot of people keep the CD in the car, or on their MP3 player, ready to deal with any upsetting thoughts and feelings that might come up.

The "Q-Work" On-line *Humenergy* Balancer
This instrument was originally designed for people doing the Radical Forgiveness process but it has proven to be equally effective for balancing *humenergy*. Being an online program, it is more interactive than the paper version of The Balancing Energy Worksheet.

A Step-by Step Process
Though very sophisticated in its design, the *Humenergy* Balancer demands no special skill, discipline or understanding on the part of the users. It requires only that people be willing to go through the simple, step-by-step process that will, by virtue of their willingness to do it and to trust the process, automatically neutralize those negative energy patterns. It's hard to believe that it would work, but it does. Go to *QEMSystem.com* and select *Online Humenergy Balancer* to experience this amazing technology. You will love it.

Benefits of QEMS to the Organization

With the installation of QEMS, a firm would expect to notice the following differences, some in the short term, others in the longer term, but significant benefits nevertheless.

• People Acting More Responsibly
More responsible behavior will be the result of what has been described in the preceding paragraphs. The changes may be imperceptible at first, but as people become more accountable to themselves and responsible for their lives, they make better decisions both for themselves and those around them. They will be seen as adding more value.

• Decreased Incidences of Hostility and Conflict
One would expect to see a dramatic decrease in hostility and incidences of conflict at all levels — between individuals, groups, departments, customers and vendors, unions and management and so on. This is probably the easiest of all improvements to measure, assuming that there has been a procedure for recording such incidents in the past.

• Less Blaming and Finger Pointing
When people become more self-accountable, they stop projecting and laying blame. It just doesn't serve them anymore because they have given up their addiction to the victim mentality that first gave rise to blaming

and projecting in the first place. They become more solution-oriented and forward looking.

• Less Covert Sabotage of Self and Others
Sabotage is very subtle and difficult to spot unless you know what to look for. It's even more difficult to quantify. One needs to look for patterns that indicate it, but the idea is that QEMS will automatically take care of it by neutralizing the underlying cause.

• Less Acting Out of Subconscious Issues
The longer QEMS is in use, the more likely it will be that unconscious *humenergy* will be neutralized. The need for it to be acted out in the workplace will therefore be eliminated.

• Marked Increase in Morale
When people begin to take responsibility for their life, they feel empowered and feel better about themselves. As people let go of blaming, complaining and whining, they look for ways to contribute. They simply feel better and contribute more.

• Greater Sense of Togetherness
If a person's energy field is in sync with the energy fields of those around them, there is attraction, caring and, ultimately, bonding. This can totally transform the atmosphere and hence the energy of a company.

HIDDEN AGENDAS **At Work**

• A More Willing and Flexible Workforce
A happier, more responsible and self-accountable workforce is likely to be more flexible, adaptable and less resistant to change than one that is self-absorbed, uncertain and dependent on the status quo. But at the same time, firms should be ready to capitalize on the desire of many to be more involved and willing to contribute in a new way.

• A Marked, Short-term Increase in Attrition Rates
Some people simply don't want to give up their victim mentality, and they become uncomfortable when the people around them begin to grow and change for the better. They usually leave within about six to twelve months, but they are quickly replaced by people with a higher vibration. That's because like attracts like. These new hires will be attracted by the high vibration of the company as a whole, and they, in turn, will contribute to raising its vibration even higher. The effect is cumulative.

• A Marked Decrease in Attrition Rates
Once the initial shake-out has occurred and the low-vibration people have been replaced by those who resonate at a higher frequency, matching that of the company as a whole, people will not leave. They will stay because they are happier and more fulfilled.

The Benefits

Bringing Racial Dissonance Into Balance
Fortunately, the Quantum Energy Management System has within its technology a way to isolate, reduce and eventually eradicate the element of race from the *humenergy* profile of the organization. Not only will this help them and the individual, but it will assist in reducing racial disharmony, prejudice and bigotry in society as a whole. The same thing could happen with sexual discrimination in the workplace.

Benefits to the 'Stealth Energy Shifter'

1. Protection from Negativity
If they work in a 'negatively charged' environment and need to protect themselves from that negativity, the Q-Work Kit tools will help a lot in this regard. The tools will enable the individuals to see that people are never upset for the reason they think, and that something of a healing nature is occurring within the situation. They wouldn't 'take on' the negative energy because they would no longer perceive it as negative.

2. More Peaceful Within
Just knowing that what is occurring is a process where negative *humenergy* is coming to the surface for healing, brings people to a state of peace about it, even when those around them are in upset. The stealth energy shifter wouldn't buy into the 'victim story,' because he/she would know that it isn't the real story.

3. Their Peace Creates More Peace
Because the stealth energy shifters are not buying into an upset or negative energy, their peaceful presence alone will shift the energy in a positive direction.

4. They Heal Their Own *Humenergy*
Stealth energy shifters are there to heal their own *humenergy* as well. For that reason they might see what's going on and judge it as negative and problematic just like everyone else. However, they might be the only ones doing their own work and the only ones recognizing it as a healing opportunity. They are also the only ones with the tools to transform that energy.

5. The Work Environment Improves Automatically
As a result of their doing the Q-Work, the energy rubs off on everyone else. This means that over time, their *humenergy* begins to get 'healed' too without the need for them to create high drama to activate it. In effect, the stealth energy shifter becomes a healer in the workplace, even without them doing or saying anything.

6. Workmates, Colleagues, and Superiors Act More Positively Towards Them
Simply as a result of what stealth energy shifters do with their own energy, the people around them complain less, become more amenable, helpful and productive. Those in a supervisory or managerial positions become more accepted and trusted by those beneath them.

7. Likely to Lead to Promotion
As their energy field becomes clearer and less susceptible to emotional stress both from within and from others, stealth energy shifters will appear to be more stable, more grounded, more dependable and so on — all the attributes that are highly valued in people moving into leadership positions. They are therefore more likely to get noticed for that kind of promotion.

8. The Top Down Effect
If the stealth energy shifters are the managers or owners of their own company and use the Q-Work tools themselves, this will have a trickle-down effect on the whole operation, even assuming no one knows that they are using it. Turnover rates will improve, so will morale, productivity and profits.

9. Opportunities to Teach Others Will Arise
The rule is that people should not share anything about QEMS until asked. They are stealth energy shifters, not missionaries, counselors or consultants. However, given time, people will begin to notice their own energy shifting and will ask them about it.

10. Other Relationships Improve
Doing the Q-Work will also improve relationships with family and others. We encourage people to share the QEMS System with their spouses and children and to have them use the tools also. Many a marriage has been saved doing this work.

How to contact us:

Websites:
 www.qemsystem.com
 www.spiritualintelligenceatwork.com
 www.radicalforgiveness.com

E-Mail: info@radicalforgiveness.com

Phone: 770-428-9181
 888-778-5696 (VM)